A Monste

The True Story of Danny Rolling
The Gainesville Ripper

by JT HUNTER

A Monster of All Time

The True Story of Danny Rolling
The Gainesville Ripper

by JT HUNTER

Copyright and Published by
RJ Parker Publishing, Inc.

ISBN-13: 978-1987902525

http://RJParkerPublishing.com/

Published in the United States of America

Copyrights

While the Publisher is responsible for the sales, marketing and distribution of a book, it is the author's obligation to ensure the accuracy of facts.

Table of Contents

Cast of Characters....5
Prologue....6
Chapter 1....8
Chapter 2....16
Chapter 3....19
Chapter 4....29
Chapter 5....32
Chapter 6....43
Chapter 7....47
Chapter 8....56
Chapter 9....62
Chapter 10....72
Chapter 11....77
Chapter 12....84
Chapter 13....88
Chapter 14....98
Chapter 15....100
Chapter 16....111
Chapter 17....123
Chapter 18....133
Chapter 19....141
Chapter 20....161
Chapter 21....183
Chapter 22....219
Chapter 23....235
Chapter 24....243
Chapter 25....254
Chapter 26....273
Appreciation....279
About the Author....280
Other Books by JT Hunter....281
RJ Parker Publishing, Inc....286

Cast of Characters

Murder Victims

Tom Grissom (55 years old)

Sean Grissom (8 years old)

Julie Grissom (24 years old)

Sonja Larson (18 years old)

Christina Powell (17 years old)

Christa Hoyt (18 years old)

Manuel Taboada (23 years old)

Tracy Paules (23 years old)

Investigators

Ray Barber, Gainesville Police Department

Gainesville Police Chief Wayland Clifton

Sadie Darnell, Gainesville Police Department and Alachua County Sheriff's Office

Lieutenant Spencer Mann, Alachua County Sheriff's Office

Gainesville Police Captain Richard Ward

Suspects

Steven Bates

Edward Humphrey

Danny Rolling

Others

Sondra London

Rod Smith, Alachua County State Attorney

Prologue

January 1987

Parchman, Mississippi

The prisoner raged in his lonely cell.

"When they let me out of here," the prisoner swore to himself, "I'll make them all pay."

Years of condemnation and contempt had taken its toll, breaking him down, eroding his spirit, destroying all sense of hope. Now only the anger remained.

~~~~~

Cast into the bowels of Parchman Prison, the notorious Mississippi State Penitentiary, the prisoner had suffered daily torments during his confinement, each day falling deeper and deeper into despair. Raw sewage regularly seeped into his cell through the floor and flowed from a broken drain down the hall, flooding the cramped 8 x 10 feet concrete space with a revolting grey-brown liquid and an unrelenting stench.

Kept in this torturous isolation, his besieged brain had betrayed him, replaying the grievous moments of his life, all of the humiliations and feelings of helplessness, every piercing word, and every raw, painful memory. It was a constant reminder that the world had always been a hurtful place of violence, animosity, and aversion, never one of empathy or understanding.

Desperate to escape the unrelenting torment, he retreated ever deeper into the labyrinth of his own mind, creeping ever closer to madness. It was in that maze of
~~~~~

insanity that he found himself. Or rather, something found him.

In the bleak, all-encompassing darkness, something whispered his name.

Faceless and formless, the voice seemed to emanate both from the impenetrable blackness surrounding him and from the shadowy depths of his own consciousness. The voice soothed and seduced him, its language both alien and familiar. It promised the strength to survive whatever nightmares awaited the remainder of his confinement. It offered the tools of revenge for his present condition, for all of the wrongs committed against him in the past, and for the scorn and mistreatment yet to come. Most of all, it promised the power to make others feel the suffering he had so long endured.

Then a name imprinted itself into his brain, uttered from an unseen shape in the darkness, or muttered from the murky depths of memory.

"Gemini," an eerie voice proclaimed. "I am Gemini."

At that moment, an infernal compact was crafted, a devil's contract offering redemption for the damned, a demonic covenant accepted regardless of the terms. Caring nothing for the consequences, the prisoner embraced the assurance of vengeance, pledging revenge for the countless injuries inflicted upon him. Just as a cold, uncaring world had robbed him of his humanity and stolen years of his life, he would take the lives of others in an equal and equitable proportion. A new sense of purpose washed over him, bringing with it a rebirth, a recognition of what he needed to do.

And now he waited, marking the days with hidden malice, the bitter darkness of his cell matched only by the malevolence of his twisted, tainted soul.

Chapter 1

Sunday, August 26, 1990

Gainesville, Florida

"*I've got a killer on the loose*" (Gainesville Police Chief Waylon Clifton)

Patricia Powell was worried. Her youngest daughter, 17-year-old Christina Powell, had recently moved into an apartment in Gainesville, a bucolic college town in central Florida about 90 minutes away from their long-time Jacksonville home. Excited to be starting her freshman year of college at the University of Florida, Christina had packed up her car and left home just a few days earlier. With classes set to begin on Monday, August 27, she and her roommate moved into their two-bedroom apartment just before the beginning of the fall semester.

Christina had called her parents around 11:05 p.m. the night of Thursday, August 23 to let them know that her roommate had arrived and that they were making good progress unpacking. Everything seemed to be going well as Christina, the baby in a family with six older siblings, took the first steps towards becoming an adult and living on her own.

When Christina did not call home on Friday, August 24, Mrs. Powell felt the normal concern of a mother not receiving an expected phone call from her child. That concern grew to outright alarm on Saturday, August 25, after Christina failed to meet her sister and brother-in-law when they arrived at her new apartment around 5:00 p.m. to deliver some furniture. Although Christina was supposed to be there to meet them, no one answered the door at the apartment. Her sister waited in the parking lot until 9:00 p.m., ultimately leaving with a mixed sense of irritation and worry, having neither seen nor heard from Christina.

Unable to ignore their increasing anxiety about Christina's well-being, Mrs. Powell and her husband made an early start on Sunday morning for the drive to Gainesville. As they pulled out of the driveway, Patricia Powell put on a brave face, but it failed to stifle the apprehensive feeling that spread from the pit of her stomach, a maternal instinct sounding an alarm, warning of something terribly wrong.

As the Powells drove south, the city of Gainesville, home to the University of Florida, the largest college in the state boasting over 30,000 students, buzzed with excitement and activity as thousands of eager young men and women arrived for the start of the new semester. Based largely on its "safe streets" and pastoral setting, *Money* magazine had named Gainesville as the 13th best place to live in the entire United States. "Have You Seen Her" by MC Hammer aired repeatedly on area radio stations and *The Exorcist III* scared audiences senseless at local movie theaters. U-Haul trucks and tightly packed cars riding low from their heavy loads filled dormitory and apartment complex parking lots, while the lines at supermarkets and department stores stretched long with new and returning students purchasing groceries and other essential supplies.

Elsewhere, another recent arrival, an emotionally-disturbed drifter, had already left his mark on the unsuspecting college town. His depraved deeds would soon turn their world upside down.

~~~~~

At 3:45 p.m. on Sunday, August 26, Gainesville Police Department officer Ray Barber responded to Christina Powell's apartment complex pursuant to a welfare check request by her parents. As he pulled into the courtyard of Williamsburg Village Apartments, a three-story residential complex located at 2000 SW 16th Street, only one mile from the University of Florida's main campus, Barber spotted the building's maintenance man waiting to meet him. After confirming the reason for the call, the two made their way to Apartment 113, which occupied the second and third floors at the rear center portion of the Kenmore building, a white,
~~~~~

mock-colonial brick structure with black and brown trim, one of eleven buildings in the apartment complex.

Officer Barber knocked loudly on the second-floor front door, the apartment's main entrance. When no one responded, the maintenance man tried opening the door with his master key, but it would not budge. The two men made their way to the rear porch door. Although locked, it appeared that the door's dead bolt could be operated from the inside by removing a small pane of glass in the door and then simply reaching in. After obtaining the manager's permission, Barber smashed the glass, but when he peered inside, he saw that the dead bolt had a double-lock design and could not be operated without a key. Failing to gain entry on the second floor, they walked up to a door on the third-floor and broke it open by dislodging it from the door frame.

Barber noticed the odor as soon as he cleared the door. It was the smell of death. He immediately drew his gun and stepped inside. It did not take long to find the source of the smell. The body of a young woman lay sprawled on her back a few feet in front of him.

Already in the initial stage of decomposition, the bloody condition of 18-year-old Sonja Larson's body showed that she had suffered a violent death. Her only item of clothing, a t-shirt pulled up past her breasts, exposed obvious stab wounds on Sonja's arm, leg, and chest, and extensive swelling on her face indicated that she had sustained a brutal blow to the head. Her arms stretched upward past her head, while her legs extended off the end of the bed, spread apart with both feet touching the floor. Multiple stab wounds were clustered on and around her right breast and a large piece of flesh appeared to have been cut from her upper left thigh, deep enough to expose the femur bone underneath. Blood was everywhere. A pool of blood discolored the center of the bed, blood-saturated pillows lay scattered at the headboard, and blood spatter stains blotched the walls closest to the bed.

A second ghastly scene awaited Barber downstairs. The nude body of another young female lay on her back on the living room floor next to a couch. It was Christina Powell. Like Sonja Larson's battered body, Christina's corpse told a tale of terror. She suffered five stab wounds to her upper back and both of her nipples had been cut off. Her neck bent toward her right shoulder and her hair fanned out from the right side of her head, deliberately placed in that position by her killer. Both of her arms extended above her head and both legs were spread wide apart, bent at the knees, fully exposing her pubic area. A nearly empty bottle of Dawn dishwashing soap had been left between her knees on top of a damp towel. The soap coated her vaginal area and left a layer of foam around her vulva. A pair of girl's underwear, apparently tossed aside by her killer, lay on the floor near her and next to the couch, beside a brown purse spotted with blood.

Marks on both victims indicated that they had been bound with tape, Christina on her wrists and Sonja on her mouth, but the tape had been removed after death by their killer. Family pictures, loose change, and the other contents of both girls' purses were dumped on the floor by Christina's body. Bloody tissue papers lay scattered around the kitchen. The rest of the apartment seemed undisturbed except for a torn, bloodstained photograph showing a black male with a white arm around him, apparently that of a white female. All of the doors to the apartment were locked with the deadbolts in place, while Sonja and Christina's cars were both undisturbed in the apartment's parking lot.

The two girls had last been seen alive around 11:00 p.m. on Thursday, August 23, when Sonja used a payphone to call home, the same phone that Christina had used to call her mom earlier that evening. After buying some items for their apartment at Wal-Mart, the two had dinner at Chili's, then stopped at a convenience store on the way back to Williamsburg Village. They planned an early morning to clean up the apartment and start looking for part-time jobs.

On the last night of their lives, Sonja went to bed upstairs wearing a yellow t-shirt with "Atlanta" on the front, while Christina slept downstairs in a yellow tank top on the couch.

~~~~~

A "happy-go-lucky kid," Sonja Larson had come to Gainesville as a National Honor Society scholar from Pompano Beach in south Florida. She took advanced classes at Ely High School, a math and science magnet school, while playing on the varsity softball team and serving as manager of the girls' basketball team. Active in the First Baptist Church of Pompano Beach, Sonja sang in the church choir, played flute in the church orchestra, led Bible study, and helped out in the church's day care center. She loved giving back to the church where she began preschool at the age of 2.

"She was great with those children," remembered Pat Hoag. "When she spoke, they listened to her. It seems like every time you saw her, she had a couple of those kids on her lap."

Sonja took summer classes at UF to gain a head start on her college studies. As a second-semester freshman, Sonja planned to major in education when classes began in the fall. Having always enjoyed working with kids, she hoped to eventually open her own day care center. Unable to secure a room in one of the university's on-campus dormitories, Sonja had settled on the Williamsburg Village apartment conveniently located just four blocks away from the college.

Sonja had met Christina Powell during summer session freshman classes when they shared the same dormitory, and the two quickly became friends. They were kindred spirits, both of them high achievers who excelled both academically and in sports in high school. Choosing to be roommates together for the fall semester had been an easy decision. On Thursday, August 23, Sonja packed up
~~~~~

her Honda CRX, bid her family a bittersweet goodbye, and made the drive north to Gainesville.

Christina Powell, called Christi by those who knew her, graduated from Episcopal High School in Jacksonville where she studied theology, worked on the school's literary magazine, and played multiple sports including softball and volleyball. Described by one of her teachers as a "fantastic, fun-loving young woman," Christi planned on becoming an architect and "couldn't wait" to start her college studies in Gainesville. She was the first member of her family to pursue a four-year college degree; the youngest of seven siblings, but the first to go to college.

Sonya Larson Grad Photo

Christina Powell

~~~~~

On Sunday, August 26, Gainesville Police Chief Wayland Clifton was enjoying a relaxing afternoon at home. He had just settled into his favorite chair to watch preseason football when the telephone rang. Silently wishing that whatever the call concerned could wait until after the game, or better yet, until Monday, Clifton lifted the phone to his ear, his eyes still following the game on the TV screen.

His Deputy Chief, Daryl Johnston, was on the line. He was at a murder scene in southwest Gainesville.

“Is it anything special?” Clifton asked, knowing full well that it must be for Johnston to be disturbing him on his day off.

“There’s two victims,” Johnston replied. “Chief, you really need to see this,” he said, the tone of his voice underscoring the urgency.
~~~~~

Clifton knew he had to go. He hung up the phone and sighed. After a last look at the Vikings-Oilers game, he grabbed a Gainesville Police Department jacket and headed out the door. When he arrived at the murder site and saw the condition of Sonja Larson's body, Clifton knew they were dealing with a "bad, bad guy."

"It was a pretty horrific scene, and I say that having been, before I became a police officer, an embalmer," Clifton would recall afterward. "I realized this was someone who was going to prey on young women, and I probably have 50,000 of them in the jurisdiction of Gainesville and Alachua County. And so I did something that is probably the last thing that police chiefs or sheriffs ever do. I decided to ask for help."

Murders were not unheard of in the growing, central Florida college town, but they were not a common occurrence, and double-homicides were extremely rare. When Clifton returned home around 3:00 a.m. on Monday morning, he called the commissioner of the Florida Department of Law Enforcement.

"I'm going to need some of your best agents," Clifton told him. "I've got a killer on the loose."

Chapter 2

1979-1982

The Deep South

In 1979, the prisoner starts down the path that leads him to Parchman Prison. Devastated when his wife serves him with divorce papers, he takes out his pain and anger on a brunette college girl living a few blocks from his house in Shreveport, Louisiana. In the middle of the night, he breaks into her house and rapes her. It is the first time that he rapes, but it will not be the last. It marks the beginning of his descent into sin, the initial decay of his soul, the first step towards true evil.

In May 1979, he robs a 7-Eleven convenience store near his home. When the frightened 7-Eleven clerk hands him the $11.00 in the cash register, he stares incredulously at the meager amount of money, and then gives it back to her stating that it is not worth keeping. Although later named as a suspect for the crime, he is never charged. He wears a ski mask so no one can identify him and he leaves no fingerprints at the scene.

The next night, he robs Charlie's Lounge, a small bar in Shreveport. After donning brown gloves and a blue ski mask, he strides into the busy bar shortly before midnight. He leaves minutes later with the contents of the bar's cash box, and again avoids any criminal charges because of the mask and a lack of fingerprints.

Feeding a romantic notion and reinforcing his self-image as being not just an outlaw, but a heroic figure on the run, the robber patterns himself after Clint Eastwood's character in his favorite film, *The Outlaw Josey Wales*. Wearing a brown sack over his head, he robs L & R Liquor in Shreveport on May 15. After demanding all of the money in the cash register, he walks out with approximately $200.

Ten days later, at 8:25 p.m. on May 25, he a Winn-Dixie grocery store in Montgomery wearing a brown ski mask and jeans. He is ca slung over his shoulder and holds a Smit' revolver in his hand. He orders the cashiers with money, then flees on foot, getting away with $800. A week later, just before 9:00 p.m., he walks into another Winn-Dixie, this one in Columbus, Georgia. Wielding the same gun and wearing the same brown ski mask, he walks to several cash registers, fills a brown grocery bag with $956 cash, and runs into a nearby woods. Half an hour later, three police officers find him hiding in some bushes. He surrenders without resisting. At the Columbus police station, he confesses to the robbery and reveals that the gun he has been using is his father's service revolver.

After pleading guilty to the Columbus robbery, he is sentenced to six years imprisonment in the Muscogee County Jail. While in jail in Georgia, he enters a guilty plea to the robbery of the Montgomery Winn-Dixie, and in August 1979, he is transferred to Georgia State Prison. Two months later, while clearing stumps as part of a work detail, the prisoner asks permission to defecate in the woods. The opportunity having presented itself, he decides to run away. Prison guards catch up to him shortly after he goes missing. A warning shot from a shotgun stops him in his tracks as he tries to run to Interstate 75.

The following year, Larry Ingram, a psychiatrist at Bryce State Hospital in Tuscaloosa, Alabama, diagnoses the prisoner with a personality disorder, an "antisocial trend," and a tendency to blame others for his problems. During another escape attempt, the prisoner suffers an injury to his right testicle at the hands of a guard with a third-degree black belt in Tae Kwon Do. The torn testicle will plague him for the rest of his life.

After earning an early release from Georgia in 1982, he is transferred to Alabama to serve two more years for the ama robbery. At the St. Clair County Jail, he is allowed cial privileges as a jail trusty. There are reduced estrictions on his movement around the grounds. In July 1982, he takes advantage of this by escaping while taking out the trash. However, police recapture him two days later in the small town of Natchidoches, Louisiana, and he serves the remainder of his sentence doing hard labor at Staton Correctional Facility back in Alabama.

Chapter 3

Monday, August 27, 1990

Gainesville, Florida

"*It could have been us*" (University of Florida student Alison Kirkpatrick)

The front-page headline of the Monday, August 27 edition of *The Gainesville Sun* proclaimed *Two UF Students Found Brutally Slain*, the first story in what would become a flood of media coverage of the case. As the news began spreading across the community, homicide investigators from the Gainesville Police Department and Alachua County Sheriff's Office gathered in a spartan conference room. The personal attendance of Sheriff Lucian Hindery, Chief Wayland Clifton, University of Florida Police Chief Everett Stevens, and State Attorney Len Register, as well as numerous commanders and detectives from the assembled law enforcement agencies, reflected the meeting's high importance. Gainesville Police Captain Richard Ward began the meeting promptly at 9:25 a.m. By then, word of mouth had ensured that all in attendance already knew why they were there, but now they would learn the lurid details.

After discussing the facts known about the double-homicide at Williamsburg Apartments, the group of investigators listened to an additional briefing, this one about a third homicide victim found only hours earlier. The murder of the third victim, 18-year-old Santa Fe Community College student Christa Hoyt, felt personal for many of those at the meeting because she worked as a clerk in the Records Bureau of the Alachua County Sheriff's Office. Indeed, Christa's body had been discovered after she failed to show up for her midnight work shift and coworkers dispatched a deputy to check on her.

Christa's supervisor, Nancy Carlton, had noticed her absence and quickly became concerned. It was wholly out of character for Christa to be a no-show at work without contacting Carlton ahead of time. Indeed, when Christa had her wisdom teeth pulled a few days earlier on Thursday, she still came to work at midnight that night. So when she failed to show up for her shift early Monday morning, Carlton asked that a deputy go by her apartment to make sure she was okay.

Deputy Keith O'Hara received the dispatch call at 1:13 a.m. on August 27. He immediately proceeded to Christa's apartment at 3533 SW 24th Avenue, less than three miles away from the Sonja Larson-Christi Powell homicide site. Located in the southeast corner of the complex, apartment M sat on the eastern side of a wood frame, grey-colored duplex building.

After announcing himself as a police officer, Deputy O'Hara knocked loudly on the front door of the apartment, but no one answered. He tried the door, but it was locked. After wandering around the building, he found the property manager in a nearby corridor, and the manager showed O'Hara how to get to the rear bedroom door of Christa's apartment. He led O'Hara through an unlocked wooden gate situated adjacent to the apartment, remarking that the gate was supposed to be latched. Then the two men walked down a narrow corridor to a chain link fence separating the building from the thick woods behind it. Seeing the manager's surprised reaction to a sagging section of the fence that seemed to have been pushed down, O'Hara ordered him to go back to the wooden gate. With the manager out of harm's way, O'Hara climbed over the sagging section of fencing and saw a sliding glass door directly in front of him. Although blinds on the door prevented him from seeing inside, they did not extend all the way down, leaving a small space between them and the ground. After laying on his stomach, Deputy O'Hara aimed his flashlight and peered into the dark apartment. What he saw was the stuff of nightmares.

Christa's headless body sat hunched forward at the edge of her bed midway between the foot of the bed and the headboard. Her hands drooped beside her thighs, which were spread wide apart, and her feet seemed to float on the floor in a pool of blood. As O'Hara stared in horror, small drops of blood continued to trickle to the floor from the decapitated torso.

Christa's head had been severed with a clean, almost surgical, cut and then placed on the top shelf of a nearby bookcase. Her head leaned against the left side of the bookcase in an upright position, propped up by a wooden jewelry box on the other side. The killer had positioned the head in such a way that Christa seemed to be staring in shock at her own body. And her head had been left where it would be the first thing anyone would see when walking into the apartment.

There were extensive injuries besides the decapitation. Narrow stab wounds were visible in Christa's back, and her torso had been mutilated as well. Both of her nipples had been cut off, and an area of flesh two inches wide was missing from her back. She had also been eviscerated. A deep cut from her pubic bone ran all the way up to the breastbone, exposing her intestines, which glistened sickeningly in the beam of O'Hara's flashlight.

O'Hara quickly called for backup and secured the scene.

~~~~~

Lieutenant Spencer Mann, Public Information Officer for the Sheriff's Office, had been asleep for just a few hours early Monday morning when the harsh ringing of his phone jarred him awake. His initial grogginess quickly melted away when he was informed that one of the sheriff's employees had been murdered. He already knew about the Sonja Larson-Christina Powell double-murder. Now Gainesville had its third murder victim in a period of two days.
~~~~~

Christa Hoyt Senior Photo

~~~~~

Crime scene investigators discovered that the latch on the sliding glass door of Christa Hoyt's bedroom had been popped off, and since there were no signs of a struggle, her killer could have been waiting for her inside the apartment when she returned home. A red-and-white Kentucky Fried Chicken box, one drumstick its only content, sat on the kitchen counter next to a Dunkin Donuts box, perhaps the remnants of Christa's last meal. An examination of Christa's body revealed tape marks on her wrists, but like the Larson-Powell homicide site, the tape had been removed and taken away by her killer. Based on the similarities between the two crime scenes, including the tape, similar knife wounds, removal of victims' nipples, and missing flesh, investigators surmised that the same person killed all three victims. Due to the more extensive body mutilation at the second crime scene, they speculated that Christi and Sonja had been the first victims, followed by Christa Hoyt.
~~~~~

Christa's killer had apparently been watching her for some time before committing the crime. The back yard of her duplex was surrounded by a nearly 7-foot fence, and the only other way into the yard was through a gate on the side of the building. Her landlord, Elbert Hoover, told police that on the afternoon of August 25, he noticed the latch on the gate was unlocked, something he observed a few days earlier as well. When he saw the unsecured gate the second time, he knocked on Christa's door to let her know since she usually kept it latched. Christa thought that the telephone repairman might have opened the gate and forgotten to secure it back. Hoover had seen a telephone company truck in the area earlier that day, so it seemed a feasible explanation. He wished Christa well and went on his way. Only after learning of the murders did he wish he had done something more.

~~~~~

Having grown up in the small town of Archer just ten miles to the southwest of Gainesville, it was natural for Christa to gravitate to the livelier college town. A popular student who "everybody liked," Christa served in the student council and performed in the school band before graduating with honors from Newberry High School the year before. Eager to be on her own, Christa moved out of her family's home shortly after her 18th birthday. Yet, despite her desire to become an adult, she "kept one foot firmly planted in childhood" by maintaining a collection of teddy bears that made the move to Gainesville with her.

"When she went to bed, she would keep them with her," recalled her stepsister, Laurie. "She slept in the middle of them all."

While working to pay the bills, Christa took classes at nearby Santa Fe Community College on scholarship as a chemistry honors student. Christa's former supervisor at a video store in Archer remembered her as "perfectionist" and a "real go-getter."
~~~~~

"She was everything I would want my daughter to be," Beverly Leduc said.

An interest in police work led her to join the Explorers unit of the Alachua County Sheriff's Office, a branch of the agency designed to allow students to get a firsthand look at law enforcement. Intrigued by the prospect of combining her interest in chemistry and police work by working at the FBI crime lab in Washington, D.C., Christa had not hesitated in taking the clerk position at the Sheriff's Office. Now that promising career in law enforcement had been viciously extinguished by an unknown killer in the night.

"I was so concerned about her living by herself and worried something like this could happen to her," Christa's stepmother, Diana Hoyt, recalled sadly. "It is something her father, her mother, and I have to think about the rest of our lives, the last hours of Christa's life."

~~~~~

Later that afternoon, results from the first two victims' autopsy reports were shared with the group of investigators. Alachua County Medical Examiner William Hamilton found that Sonja Larson had suffered eleven stab wounds to her right arm, clearly indicating that she had tried to defend herself from a brutal attack. She also had five stab wounds tightly clustered around her right nipple, two stab wounds to the left side of her chest, and a large incised wound on her left leg. The stab wounds all ranged from 1 to 2 ½ inches in length, and the wounds to Sonja's right breast, which had been inflicted through her t-shirt, included punctures of her right lung and the right atrium of her heart. Her left lung suffered a "deep stab wound" and a two-inch "slice of spleen was incompletely sliced away."

Although Christina Powell had fewer puncture wounds, they proved just as deadly. Five stab wounds through her back measured similar to Sonja's, 1 1/8 inches to 1 7/8 inches in length, and at least two of those punctured her right lung. Hamilton confirmed Christi's probable cause
~~~~~

of death to be "multiple stab wounds" to her back "with perforation of aorta, left lung and heart". He estimated that Christi had remained alive for one to two minutes after the fatal stabbing. He also noted a "sticky gray-white fluid" coating her pubic hair and vagina, apparently the result of her killer's efforts to eliminate any semen evidence from being left behind for the police to find.

While the homicide investigators discussed the results of his examination of Christi and Sonja, Hamilton completed his autopsy of Christa Hoyt. He found eleven stab wounds to her left arm, five wounds clustered around her right nipple, two on the left side of her chest, and a "large incised wound' on her left leg. He pronounced Christa's probable cause of death to be a stab wound that penetrated her back and extended 7 ½ inches in length, piercing her aorta, lung, and heart.

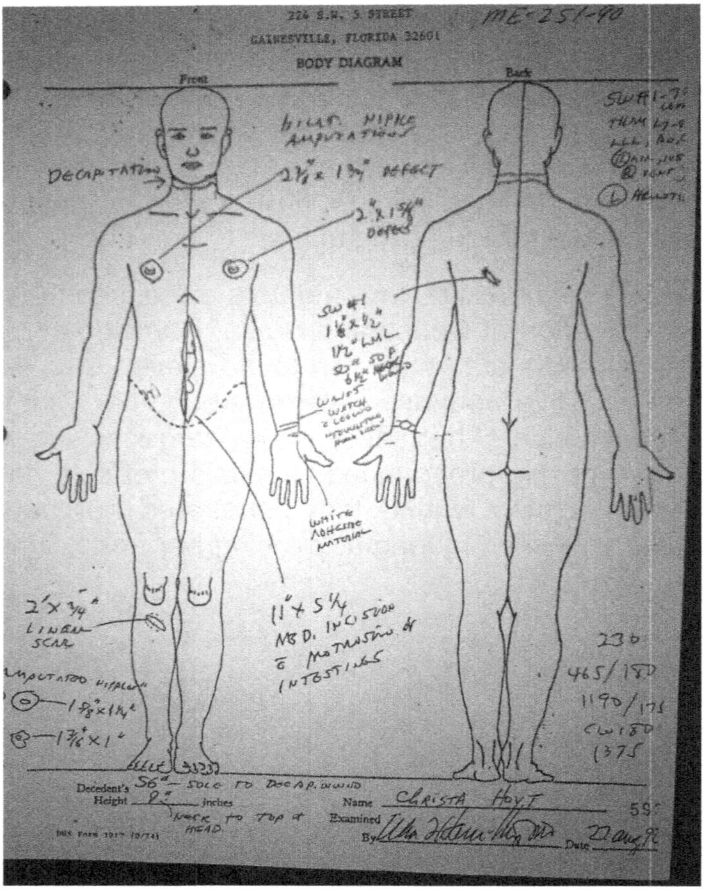

Christa Hoyt Autopsy Diagram

~~~~~

As the initial stages of the investigation got underway, detectives began organizing and following up the countless leads already being called in. A man who lived near Christa Hoyt's apartment complex reported seeing two black males walking towards the area of Christa's apartment just after midnight on the date of her murder. Around the same time, a Publix employee reported encountering a tall, white male with sandy-blonde hair as he drove home from work. When the beams of his headlights lit up the unknown individual, he
~~~~~

quickened his pace and ducked behind a dumpster area in front of Christa's apartment complex. The "dirty, junky" looking man kept his face hidden from the witness the entire time. Yet another witness driving by the apartment building reported seeing a white male about six feet tall with medium length blonde hair walking toward the building around 10:00 p.m. the previous night. The list of possible suspects quickly grew long without anyone standing out as the most promising lead.

Christi Powell's sister informed investigators that Christi's boyfriend, a black male named Adrian White, had driven with her from St. Augustine to Gainesville on the night of Wednesday, August 22, a revelation which immediately made him a person of interest in the case. In addition, detectives discovered a letter from Sonja Larson's boyfriend, a college student in Tennessee, expressing his hurt, disbelief, and anger in response to her decision to break up with him. The letter pointed to an obvious motive for her murder.

Although neither victim had been seen on Friday the 24th, Sonja and Christi's neighbors reported hearing their shower running around 6:30 a.m. that morning, highly unusual since neither of the girls were early risers. In addition, their next-door neighbor heard George Michael's song, "Faith," playing loudly in their apartment a few hours later at 10:00 a.m. Since the medical examiner placed their times of death before both events, investigators surmised that their killer had been cleaning up and felt in no hurry to leave the crime scene. One detective speculated that the killer had a specific reason for selecting "Faith" to play, intending the song to convey some sort of message to the police.

Along with the numerous reports about suspicious figures spotted in the vicinity of the crime scenes, more fantastical tips flooded police phone lines as well. Carol Jackson, a psychic who helped solve a series of child murders in Atlanta, called to advise that she believed the killer to be in his mid-twenties to thirties, with reddish blonde or brown hair, an average build, and a scar on his lip. In her vision of the suspect, she saw him working in the food service industry wearing a uniform to make deliveries. Similarly, Debra Sharp called to share a dream she had in which the killer hung his victims up like meat and skinned them in a round, steel building. In her dream, the name "Donald Green" appeared along with the numbers "333".

~~~~~

Media coverage of the murders drastically intensified after the discovery of Christa Hoyt's body, no doubt fueling the surge of leads being phoned in to police as the large student population at the University of Florida and other Gainesville residents became gripped by the fear of an unknown killer in their midst. For many, the murders revived nearly forgotten memories of young co-eds savagely attacked in another Florida college town over a decade earlier. In 1978, infamous serial killer Ted Bundy had killed two Florida State University students in their Chi Omega sorority house in Tallahassee and brutally assaulted another student in a residence off campus. After being caught, convicted, and sentenced to death, Bundy had lived on Death Row for many years and had only recently been executed, put to death in Florida's electric chair on January 24, 1989. Now the ghost of Bundy haunted a new college town as the specter of another serial killer spread a shroud of terror across Gainesville.
~~~~~

Chapter 4

1985-1986

Mississippi

Having completed his Alabama sentence, the convict hitchhikes through Mississippi in June 1985. He is enjoying a ride when the car that picked him up is pulled over by the local police. The police arrest the driver for driving under the influence, but before they take him away, he asks the convict to take care of his .45 handgun that is stored in the glove compartment. It is a crime of opportunity, and the convict takes advantage of the situation by stealing the gun.

On July 22, 1985, the convict uses the stolen gun to rob a Kroger grocery store in Clinton, Mississippi. Wearing a black ski mask and gloves, he walks through the store's shopping cart door at 10:10 p.m., and bellows "This is a hold up!" He approaches the closest Kroger cashier, James Lansdale, and tells him to "put the money in the bag." Lansdale initially laughs off the command, thinking that some of his friends are playing a joke on him. But the robber is not laughing. He points his gun at the confused cashier and repeats in a hostile tone: "Put the money in the bag now." Realizing it's not a joke, Lansdale quickly complies and empties his register of almost $300. Bag in hand, the robber runs out the same door back into the parking lot. Another employee subsequently tells police that the robber had asked him the time earlier that night while he was stocking one of the store's shelves.

The robber is arrested early the next morning when Clinton police catch him driving a tan 1984 Ford LTD that had been reported stolen by its owner less than an hour earlier. The robber had broken into the home of Neil Prime by smashing a glass pane in the back door. Then he took the car keys from the kitchen table and drove off with the vehicle. According to the arrest report:

On 7-23-85 at 0338 hours, Officer Hurst observed a vehicle which gained Officer Hurst's attention by stopping suddenly on Springridge Road and Spanish Oak Drive. Officer Hurst then followed the Suspect vehicle west on Spanish Oak Drive . . . The Suspect vehicle then turned 180 degrees around and traveled westbound on Casa Grande and stopped at Los Pueblos. Officer Hurst stopped behind the Suspect vehicle.

At the time the Suspect exited the Suspect vehicle and approached Officer Hurst's vehicle. Officer Hurst requested a driver's license from the Suspect and asked the Suspect to place his hands on Officer Hurst's vehicle.

When three other patrol units arrived at the scene, Officer Hurst observed . . . a ski mask on the passenger seat. At that time the Officers inquired as to the Suspect's reason for being in the area. The Suspect then stated, "I'll tell you what you want to know." The Suspect was read his rights and at that time verbally waived his right. The Suspect then stated that he had just stolen the vehicle which he was driving. The Suspect further stated that he had committed the armed robbery which had occurred at the Kroger on the previous evening.

. . . . .

The Suspect then led officers to an area approximately 150 feet west of Clinton-Raymond Road in a wooded area where the gun, $289.55 stolen in the robbery and his personal belongings were found.

As his reason for committing the crimes of armed robbery, house burglary, and auto theft, the robber states simply: "I hadn't eaten in two days. I was hungry."

The robber appears for his March 20, 1986, trial with shaved eyebrows and tells the judge to cut off his hands so that he will not be able to commit any more robberies. He pleads guilty to grand larceny for the Kroger robbery and is sentenced to four years in the Mississippi correctional system. At the Hinds County detention center, a clerk calls the prisoner's father to find out what he wants to do to help his son. In response, the prisoner's father screams expletives into the phone and viciously admonishes the clerk. He tells the clerk to never contact him again about his "S.O.B." son. The clerk is shocked by the father's reaction. The prisoner is not.

On April 14, 1986, the prisoner escapes from the Hinds County Jail by swimming across the Snake River. Six days later, deputies question him when they see him walking along I-10 in El Paso, Texas. After first identifying himself as Jesse Mitchell, the escapee eventually gives them his real name. He is arrested and extradited back to Mississippi. This time he is sent to Parchman Prison.

Chapter 5

August 28, 1990

Gainesville, Florida

"It was an atmosphere of almost tangible fear" (FDLE Agent J.O. Jackson)

On the morning of Tuesday, August 28, 1990, the multi-agency group of homicide investigators assembled again. Two more bodies had been found. And this time one of the victims was a male. Manuel Taboada and Tracy Paules, both 23-year-old UF students, were discovered in their residence at Gatorwood Apartments, a 240-unit complex located a block west of 34th Street and about a mile from Christa Hoyt's home. Both victims had been stabbed to death. Manny Taboada's murder had been especially bloody due to dozens of stab wounds across his body.

Manny Taboada

Tracy Paules Senior Photo

Shortly before 7:00 a.m. that morning, student Tommy Carroll had gone to Gatorwood Apartments to check on Manny and Tracy at the request of a mutual friend who lived out of town. The building manager sent a maintenance man to accompany Carroll to Manny and Tracy's apartment, number 1203. After knocking on the front door elicited no response, the maintenance man used his master key to unlock it. As soon as he opened the door, he saw Tracy's body lying in the hallway between the apartment's two bedrooms. A dark-colored bag was beside her head. He immediately slammed the door shut and relocked it. When he returned five minutes later with the police, the door was unlocked and the bag was gone. Police found Manny's bloodied body inside his bedroom.

~~~~~

Friends since high school, Tracy and Manny had decided to share an apartment because Tracy wanted the security of living with a male roommate. She felt that it would be safer than living with another female.
~~~~~

"She moved in with Manny so he could be her protector," Tracy's grieving father, George Paules, would say later.

Tracy had good reason to think that way. Standing 6'2" and weighing a solid 200 pounds, Manny had played offensive guard at American High School in Hialeah near Miami. But he was far from the stereotypical dumb jock. He also served as president of the school's drama club and played the lead male role in *Grease*. At the same high school, Tracy had been a cheerleader, softball player, newspaper editor, senior class president, and homecoming queen. Her senior class had voted her "Best All-Around."

"They were dream kids," their former principal, Fred Bertani, said. "The kind of kids every parent wanted their kids to be."

After high school, Manny and Tracy worked while taking classes at Miami-Dade Community College and eventually decided to move to Gainesville. Manny planned to become an architect and had been accepted into architectural school. Tracy intended to go to law school after finishing her prelaw studies at UF.

The summer before the move to Gainesville, Tracy lived with her parents and older sister in Miami. During that last summer of her life, she worked for a law firm where co-workers described her as "breathtakingly beautiful." Near the end of August, Tracy loaded up her charcoal-grey Toyota Corolla, squeezing one last box into the backseat leaving just enough space to shove the door closed.

"There was more stuff packed in that car than you could get in a moving van," her father remembered later with a mournful smile.

Tracy planned on staying the weekend with her new boyfriend, Khris Pascarella, at his parents' house in Merritt Island, before continuing on to her new apartment in Gainesville.

"Neither of us is going to cry, right?" she asked her mom, wiping away the beginnings of a tear.

"Right," Ricky Paules murmured, her eyes watering as well, "now get out of here."

Tracy climbed into her car, started the engine, and slowly backed out of the driveway. Then she stopped and drove up again. Mother and daughter shared a long hug.

"I love you, Mom," Tracy said. "You know I couldn't leave without saying goodbye."

Amidst a few more tears, Tracy pulled into the street and drove away. Ricky Paules watched as Tracy's car grew smaller in the distance and then disappeared from view.

A few days later, on the night of Sunday, August 26, Tracy called home from her new apartment in Gainesville. After asking about her weekend at Merritt Island, Tracy's mother told her that two young women's bodies had been found in the area earlier that afternoon. Ricky Paules implored her daughter to be careful and to stay close to Manny.

Her father joked around to cope with the worry and sadness of separation.

"Boy, am I glad you're out of here!" he exclaimed. "Now I can get my parking space back and I don't have to walk through a bunch of shit in the bedroom!"

They shared a laugh, then said their goodbyes.

"I love you, Tracy," her father said.

"I love you too, Daddy," Tracy replied before hanging up the phone.

Shortly afterward, Tracy chatted on the phone with Lisa Buyer, a friend from Fort Lauderdale who had called her around midnight. Tracy and Lisa's 45-minute conversation focused on a trip to Captiva they were planning for the following weekend, but they also talked about the three student murders.

"You need to be careful," Lisa cautioned her friend, "the killer's still on the loose."

"I'll be okay," Tracy assured her, "I have Manny."

Having the hulking former football player there relieved some of Lisa's anxiety, but she still worried about her friend.

"Call me tomorrow morning," she insisted.

"Okay. I love you," Tracy said before hanging up around 12:50 a.m.

Manny Taboada came home late that night, arriving around 1:45 a.m. from his new job as a bartender at Bennigan's, just down Archer Road from Gatorwood Apartments. He had done so well on Bennigan's pre-employment test that he landed the bartender job without having to undergo the usual prerequisite of serving tables or being a bar helper.

Standing unseen in the woods behind the apartment, a dark figure had been watching Tracy through the window. He saw her hang up the phone and get ready for bed. He heard the rumble of Manny's motorcycle in the parking lot followed by the clack of the apartment door closing. He was still watching when Manny poked his head into Tracy's bedroom to say goodnight before heading to his own bedroom and falling into bed exhausted. The watcher in the woods waited a few minutes longer after Tracy turned out the light in her bedroom. Then he stepped out of the shadows and crept silently toward her.

~~~~~

Around 2:30 a.m., the piercing sound of a woman's scream jolted David Leroy awake. Leroy's girlfriend had called him three hours earlier asking him to come over and
~~~~~

spend the night because she was afraid to be alone with a killer on the loose. She lived in apartment 1207, directly above Tracy and Manny's place. Leroy had not hesitated in walking over from his apartment at Williamsburg Village to his girlfriend's place at Gatorwood. Upon arriving at Gatorwood around midnight, he noticed a white male wearing a backpack standing next to the basketball hoop. He did not think twice about it since backpacks were commonly carried in the college town at all hours of the night. Leroy continued on to his girlfriend's apartment and they watched TV until about 12:30 a.m., then went to bed.

The scream that abruptly awakened Leroy just as suddenly went silent. Still, it was enough to prod him into getting up and having a look around. He checked on his girlfriend's roommates, who were both sound asleep in their bedrooms. Then he peered out the windows, walked out onto the balcony, and listened for any other sounds. Not seeing or hearing anything suspicious, he went back to bed.

Worried about her friend's safety, Lisa Buyer repeatedly tried to reach her by phone on Monday, August 27. When Tracy failed to return Lisa's calls on Tuesday the 28th, Buyer called their mutual friend, Tommy Carroll, and begged him to check on her. That was how Tracy and Manny's bodies were found.

~~~~~

Although similar to the other two murder sites in many ways, the Gatorwood crime scene differed in one significant respect: neither body at Gatorwood had been mutilated. The lack of mutilation of either Manny or Tracy's body, combined with the locked-then-unlocked door and disappearing bag, led investigators to conclude that the killer had been interrupted before he could complete his plans. He had gained entry to Manny and Tracy's apartment through the rear dining room door on the second floor. Fresh pry marks on the door frame showed where the killer had forced it open.
~~~~~

Alachua County Medical Examiner William Hamilton conducted the autopsy of Tracy Paules on the evening of August 28. In addition to three stab wounds, he noted a "light coating of liquid soap present on the pubic and perianal region." He concluded that Tracy died from blood loss, finding "multiple stab wounds of back with penetration of left lung . . . and pulmonary aspiration of blood." Based on her injuries, Hamilton opined that after infliction of the stab wounds, it would have taken between two and five minutes for Tracy to go into irreversible shock and die.

The news of the third murder scene spread quickly across the University of Florida campus. Under the headline *Lust Killer Toll Now 5 – Hundreds Leave UF*, the August 29 edition of the *Orlando Sentinel* reflected other area newspapers in describing a mass exodus of students fleeing the school in fear.

"We're going to pack tonight and go home," said Liana Blanco, a senior. "It's just too scary here. Our parents won't let us stay."

"I don't want to be here if there's a crazy guy running around killing people," student Ali Dewing said. "Everybody's pretty much going home."

"We're not just waiting around to see who's next," echoed 21-year-old John Hoffman, carrying a golf club for protection as he escorted his roommate and girlfriend to their car.

Those who stayed became hyper-vigilant about their safety amidst the anxiety and uncertainty of not knowing when or where the killer would strike next. Students like 17-year-old freshman Gayle Hartsig slept on the floor in friends' rooms so that they would not have to sleep alone. Hartsig and her roommate learned of the murders from her mom, who cried hysterically as she relayed the news. Like hundreds of other students, Hartsig fled home Labor Day weekend and, although she returned to campus after the holiday, her roommate stayed away the entire next week. Some of her friends never returned to the campus again.

The residents of the tranquil college town that had counted only one student murder in the past three years struggled to comprehend the stunning news that five students' bodies had been discovered in a span of three days. Just as disturbing to the collective social psyche, students who had previously believed themselves to be invincible experienced the next few days as a blur, trying to come to terms with the knowledge of their new-found mortality.

When we're young we believe we're invincible and immortal. Nothing can really hurt us. Death is just a dream, some hazy, nebulous concept so remote and unthreatening that it holds no power over us. Murder is something we hear about on the news, something that happens to others, something that takes place somewhere else. The idea that it could happen to us is so alien as to be virtually inconceivable. The five young victims no doubt shared that same feeling of invincibility until the sickle of death suddenly appeared in their darkened apartments. The apparently random murders of five young college students forced a fundamental change of perspective for their fellow students, annihilating their entire sense of self, life, and reality.

During the long nights and dark days that followed, panicked students and other frightened Gainesville residents bought out the city's supply of dead bolts, stun guns, Mace, shotguns, rifles, and baseball bats.

"I've never seen anything like this before," said Butch Ford, owner of Sapp's Pawn and Gun Shop. "But I've never seen five murders in Gainesville in 48 hours."

Despite the overwhelming fear, Police Chief Clifton cautioned against buying weapons.

"Vigilantism is never good," he warned. "Usually what you get is an innocent person being hurt."

Scared residents did not heed Clifton's calls for caution. Instead, they stormed the county's gun stores scooping up rifles and shotguns to avoid the 48-hour waiting period required for handguns. Students huddled together at night and avoided going out alone. Some were too scared to turn on a light lest it attract the killer's attention. One student's concerns encapsulated the mood of the community.

"Why aren't they telling us anything?" she asked, her voice trembling with fear and frustration. "I just want to know how he's getting in. I'm scared. I didn't even sleep at my house last night."

As dismayed residents struggled to make sense out of the senseless killings, rumors fueled by hysteria spread through the community like wildfire. One contended that the killer was a pizza deliveryman, a rumor that nearly drove local pizza places out of business. Another claimed that the killer was impersonating police officers, which considerably impeded detectives' efforts to interview wary residents. There was, FDLE agent J.O. Jackson later recalled, "an atmosphere of almost tangible fear."

With an unknown serial killer stalking the streets of Gainesville, the shadow of an infamous but long-dead killer loomed large across Alachua County, spawning more speculation and panic.

"That's what we're all saying – it's another Ted Bundy on the loose," said Jana Walters, an 18-year-old UF freshman.

"I've heard people say it's like he's come out of the grave," remarked Angie Tipton, a spokesman for the UF Police Department.

Terrified students even began to suspect each other.

"I think the killer's a student," 26-year-old medical student Sonja Peterson asserted. She lived in an apartment just down from the Larson-Powell murder scene. "The murders started right when school was starting," Peterson added. "And it would be hard to fit in if you were a 40-year-old psycho-looking guy."

"I've started noticing guys and thinking, 'Oh my God, it could be him,'" said 21-year-old junior Lisamarie O'Leary. "All of a sudden every guy looks like a murderer."

The telephones at the Gainesville Police Department and Alachua County Sheriff's Office came alive every night with nervous callers reporting anyone suspicious and anything alarming, from what looked like a man's shadow on the wall to the sound of metal scraping on a door. No one felt safe with a "methodical maniac" roaming the streets in the dark of the night. Anyone could be the next victim because no one knew for sure how the killer chose his prey.

"Everybody's walking around in a daze," 19-year-old Michelle Jones noted. "They've got bags under their eyes. They're terrified."

Even seasoned members of law enforcement had difficulty coping. Aside from the inherent stress of working multiple homicides, the bloody, disturbing crime scenes and the macabre posing of the murder victims left traumatic impressions on the investigators who viewed them.

"I can vividly recall them in my mind even now," Lt. Spencer Mann, spokesperson for the Alachua County Sheriff's Office, would recall decades later. Like many others who worked the crime scenes, Mann had nightmares for months afterward and needed counseling to help deal with what he witnessed.

"I've been to a lot of deaths over the years," he said, "but these clearly were the most horrific ones I'd ever seen."

Mann's counterpart in the Gainesville Police Department, Lt. Sadie Darnell, expressed a similar reaction.

"It was a much different murder scene than I had ever experienced before," she explained. "It was an eerie feeling and very much a feeling of the presence of evil. That all sounds so trite, I know, but it was a feeling I had never had before. The only thing that could have caused that was something that was evil."

Indeed, the savage nature of the slayings presented lurid proof that something evil stalked the streets of Gainesville. As Criminologist Ron Holmes recalled, "the outstanding thing I see is the rage expressed. So many killings in such a short period of time. It looks like utter hatred and rage directed toward young women."

Chapter 6

1986

Parchman, Mississippi

Deemed an escape risk, the prisoner begins his sentence in Unit 27 of Parchman Prison on May 4, 1986. In October, he petitions for a transfer to another unit of the prison on grounds he has been threatened by several other inmates because he is a police officer's son and believes that his "life is in danger". As a result, he is transferred into administrative segregation in Unit 24, but a few months after being reassigned, one of the guards moves him to a cell at the end of the oldest part of the prison. The guard has a grudge against him because his transfer request displaced a long-time inmate who the guard had befriended. The guard retaliates by moving him to one of the worst cells in the prison in the middle of winter.

So begins the prisoner's stint of solitary confinement in the "hell-hole" of bitter cold, roaches, rats, and raw sewage that sows the seeds of murder in his soul. He endures the harsh conditions for eight months, remaining there through the summer of 1987, locked in the cell 24 hours a day except for occasional showers. His only companions are three spiders lurking in their webs in one corner of the ceiling. One day he kills two of them in a fit of anger. The prisoner serves three years of his four-year sentence before being paroled on July 29, 1988.

After getting out of Parchman Prison, he moves back into his parents' house in Shreveport. In September 1988, he meets 55-year-old Lillian "Bunnie" Mills when his father invites her to the family home for dinner. When Mills walks in the door, the convict remarks "how beautiful" she looks and proclaims that her beauty has "stopped his heart". After dinner, they take turns playing Mills's guitar. They start seeing each other frequently over the following weeks and by November 1988 their friendship has blossomed into a romantic relationship. They have what Mills describes as "plain old sex" about once a week. He never asks or forces her to do anything unusual. He is "always a nice guy" around her and never acts violent in any way, but he does behave "very child-like" and often does not "act his age." She likens him to a teenager prone to taking unnecessary risks. They will date off and on for three years.

From October 1988 through April 1989, he works at Western Sizzler restaurant, Walmart, and Circle K, not staying at any of them more than a month or two. In June 1989, he takes a job at Pancho's Mexican Buffet in Shreveport. There he meets Diane Mays, a petite brunette, who finds him to be "friendly" and "nice". He wants a serious relationship, but she is not ready, having recently separated from her ex-husband.

On November 4, he is fired from Pancho's for failing to come to work the preceding three days despite his claim that someone changed the schedule. Furious for what he perceives to be an unjust termination, he "makes a big scene in front of customers" and threatens the manager.

Mills convinces Truman Cooley, an electrician friend of hers, to hire the convict in March 1990. He works there for three weeks before being laid off due to lack of customers. Cooley finds him to be "an extremely hard worker" and would "not hesitate" to hire him again.

During their time together, the convict tells Mills that his father had humiliated him during his marriage to Omatha by coming into their bedroom, jerking the covers off of him while he was naked in bed, and holding a knife to his throat in front of his wife.

He struggles to deal with constantly being "condemned & criticized" by his father and Mills views him as "unstable" and "being like a child" emotionally. He often talks about the fact that he loves his father, but that he can never please him.

"How can I ever be somebody?" he asks, "I want to so bad. I've always wanted to make my dad proud of me, even though I know he caused me to be the way I am."

Mills believes that he "carries complex fear and guilt" and "deep seeded" [*sic]* anxieties from childhood, "not knowing how to cope, but wanting so desperately to fit into society." After much begging and pleading, Mills convinces him to see a psychiatrist, and she drives him to the Shreveport Mental Health Clinic, but he resents being analyzed by the psychiatrist and terminates the session.

~~~~~

At her deposition many years later, Mills would be asked whether she thought her boyfriend had the capacity to commit murder:

> Q. Was there anything in [his] behavior that suggested to you that he could commit homicide?
>
> A. No. No. And when the task force came to my house, if they had told me they had come there to talk about murder, I would have said, "You're at the wrong place," because there's no way that I could conceivably see [him] doing this.

~~~~~

On April 27, 1990, he is in a serious car accident during a severe storm. He is on his way home from Superior Bar & Grill at the same time that meteorologists issue a tornado warning for the area. In a freak occurrence, his car hydroplanes at the same time a powerful gust of wind hits it, propelling the car over 12 feet into the air and smashing it against the top of a telephone pole. Ejected from the car, he is knocked unconscious after injuring his head on impact.

After recovering from the car accident, he resumes peeping into windows at night, a habit he began as a teenager, but does more frequently now. Then he begins breaking into houses. From there, his behavior escalates to burglaries and rapes. In Bossier City, Louisiana, he breaks into a trailer with a woman and baby inside. He has a knife, mask, and duct tape with him. As he tries to subdue the woman, she grabs at the knife blade. As the blade cuts her hand, she manages to slip away from him and run out the door. In Shreveport, he sexually assaults a woman and steals a .38 revolver from her. He also rapes a 17-year-old after taping her hands and eyes with duct tape. He rapes another woman in Savannah, Georgia. He enjoys being in complete control of his victims and becomes addicted to the excitement of the experiences.

Chapter 7

August 29, 1990

Gainesville, Florida

"I've never been associated with a crime scene that had so many violent attacks and so little evidence left behind. This is not your average criminal." (Forensic expert Michael West)

By August 29, newspapers around the country carried coverage of the killings, with national newspapers like *The Washington Post* and *The New York Times* featuring headlines such as *Serial Killings of Five Students Terrorize Florida College Town* and *Panic on Florida Campus After 5 Are Slain*. Across Florida, a leading headline from the *United Press International* proclaimed, *Killer sought petite, brown-haired women*, an announcement causing countless brunettes in Alachua County and surrounding areas to dye their hair to a different color.

"We're still trying to find if there's any common denominator or commonalities between the five victims," Police Chief Wayland Clifton said. "Dark hair seems to be one of the commonalities. Obviously, he likes young people," Clifton added.

"We don't know who he is," said department spokesperson Sadie Darnell. "He may appear as normal as you or I except he murders people. We're nowhere near saying we've got a suspect, but we're very encouraged with the cooperation we're getting."

Gainesville investigators found numerous evidentiary connections among the three crime scenes. All three scenes shared remarkable similarities both in terms of the killer's method of entry and his acts against the victims before, during, and after the murders. In all three cases, the killer gained entry to the victims' apartments through rear doors at dimly lit areas of the buildings late at night or during the early pre-dawn hours. All three scenes also involved a victim who had been sexually assaulted and bound with tape at the mouth or wrists prior to the sexual assault. The tape had been removed and taken from the scene by the killer in all three locations as well. At the first crime scene, Christi Powell had a tight pattern of stab wounds near the center of her back. Christa Hoyt and Tracy Paules had similar wounds at the second and third crime scenes, respectively. All of the victims were killed by the same type of long-bladed knife, and all of the rape victims' shirts and bras were cut off during the assaults. The purses of the female victims were dumped out and the killer looked through the contents at all three crime scenes. In addition, all four of the female victims were white females, college students, under the age of 23, about five feet four inches tall, with shoulder-length brown or dark hair. And aside from Christa Hoyt, who had been decapitated and cut open from pelvis to breast, all of the female victims had been posed with their legs spread apart and their arms extended above their heads. Prints had been difficult to find at all three scenes and detectives theorized that the killer likely wore gloves while committing the crimes.

Other commonalities included that the killer used soap and towels to clean up evidence of sexual assault at the first and third crime scenes, and the first and second locations involved the infliction of post-mortem wounds or mutilation to the female victims. Investigators speculated that the killer did not inflict such post-mortem injuries to Tracy Paules at the third crime scene because he took the time to rape her both before and after killing her, and thus may have been interrupted and forced to flee before he wanted to leave. Seemingly less significant and apparently random characteristics shared among the crime scenes included that victims at all three locations were killed on water beds and all three apartments had a house cat that was unharmed and present when officers arrived.

Having analyzed the crime scenes, Capt. Richard Ward concluded that they were all "packaged in such a way as to make some sort of statement. The person doesn't necessarily want you to say *why?* as much as he wants you to be shocked by the *way* he committed the crime."

Spencer Mann of the Alachua County Sheriff's Office tried to assure the public that his agency's resources were devoted to finding the killer.

"I don't think it takes a rocket scientist to figure out that anybody that commits homicide using mutilation is a pretty sick individual and it's somebody we want to get off the streets very badly," Mann said.

But the magnitude of the case demanded the attention of more than one police department. Due to the complexity of the investigation, the panic already spreading through the community, and the need to find the killer before he claimed another victim, the Alachua County Sheriff's Office and Gainesville Police Department combined their resources to form a special task force devoted to identifying and finding the killer of the five Gainesville students. In addition to 40 officers and deputies from the two local police departments, the Student Homicide Task Force would be augmented with extra investigators and crime scene analysts from the Florida Department of Law Enforcement as well as investigators from the State Attorney's Office. FBI profilers would also travel from Quantico, Virginia, to provide a likely personality profile of the "shrewd" and "methodical" killer. The largest of its kind in Florida history, the task force would eventually include the efforts of 180 law enforcement officers and involve a total cost of approximately $6 million.

~~~~~

On the morning of August 29, Medical Examiner William Hamilton conducted the autopsy of Manny Taboada. Hamilton noted the "blood-soaked garments" on Manny's body consistent with the "total of 31 cuts and stabs on [his] face, trunk, arms and right leg." A major stab wound on the
~~~~~

left side of his chest had an “internal wound track about 6” long going from front to back, from left to right, and slightly downward passing through left chest wall, upper lobe of left lung, ascending aorta, superior vena cava and terminates in the lower lobe of the right lung.” In addition to that major wound, Manny suffered “multiple punctures of right and left lungs from other stab wounds” as well. Thirteen of the stab wounds were to his hands, reflecting the fierce fight he put up trying to fend off his attacker. The “multiple stab wounds” causing Manny’s death included cuts and stabs to his face, neck, chest, abdomen, arms, right leg, lungs, stomach, and aorta. The extent of Manny’s injuries was truly horrific.

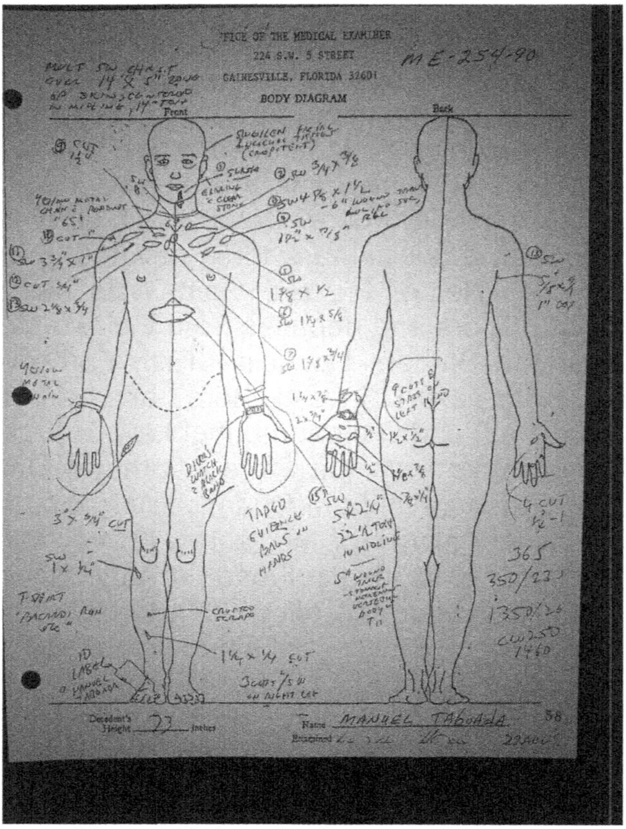

Manny Taboada Autopsy Diagram

Later that afternoon, task force leaders gathered in Captain Ward's office at the Gainesville Police Department to meet with renowned criminal profilers, FBI Special Agents Jim Wright and John Douglas. The group's discussion focused on a promising new suspect who had been identified during a canvass of neighborhoods surrounding the crime scenes. One interview in particular from that canvass raised red flags in the eyes of investigators. Several residents of the Gatorwood Apartments complex revealed that they had kicked their ex-roommate out of the apartment the week before because he "was acting crazy". They described the former roommate as a "loner" who had scars on his face and a gouge on his leg, both remnants of a severe car accident. According to the witnesses, this individual had a habit of putting on military-style camouflage clothes after midnight and going on what he referred to as "stake outs," usually not returning until the early morning hours. According to the man's ex-roommates, he was also upset over the fact that his girlfriend had recently broken up with him, and they pointed out that the girlfriend "looked just like" several of the female victims in the recent murders.

An imposing figure standing over 6 feet tall and weighing about 230 pounds, the suspect certainly had the physical strength needed to overpower the five victims. He met other important criteria attributed to the killer as well. He frequently carried a large hunting knife strapped to his leg, and his former roommates emphasized that he "hates women". A background check revealed that he had received psychiatric treatment in mental institutions and had been diagnosed as paranoid/schizophrenic. His behavior in recent days also reflected mental instability. Indeed, just the day before, he had appeared at his old high school in Melbourne, Florida, acting disoriented and "strung-out." Additionally, witnesses noticed that he had a bandage on his right hand, as if he had recently been cut by a knife.

The suspect had moved into the Gatorwood Apartments complex in June, and he lived in a building across the parking lot from Tracy Paules and Manny Taboada. Moreover, shortly before their murders, he had been seen staring at Tracy.

"He had a major crush on Tracy," said Rachel Oliver, a Gatorwood resident who knew her. "He tried to get her attention at the pool by staring at her, smiling at her, inviting her to sit with him while he drank beer. He'd fall over himself to be near her or to help her. He'd go and sit by the pool and watch when she'd come out."

Oliver had shivered when she saw him, as if the icy fingers of a cold hand were caressing her spine.

"That boy was fierce – he really scared me," she recalled with a shudder. "You could tell by the look in his eyes that he was fierce and totally crazy."

Captain Ward cautioned that all leads needed to be investigated, but after being briefed about the new suspect, FBI profiler John Douglas told the investigative team that he "fits the crimes and the profile" of the killer. Eager to solve the case, the task force began around-the-clock surveillance monitoring the whereabouts of Edward Humphrey, a 19-year-old, part-time University of Florida student, who was now the prime suspect in five bloody murders.

~~~~~

Although Edward Humphrey had not been publicly named as a suspect, his identification infused task force members with new energy. They were excited by the prospect of apprehending the killer, and eager to put a depraved criminal behind bars. The day after Tracy Paules and Manny Taboada's bodies were found, police in a night stalker surveillance plane followed Humphrey as he drove from Gainesville to his grandmother's house in Indialantic, a small city near Melbourne on Florida's east coast. Former neighbors described Humphrey as "scarred mentally as well as physically," and further investigation revealed that he had a history of threatening people with his knife, including
~~~~~

warning a security guard at Gatorwood Apartments that "God told me to kill you." Other acts by Humphrey raised additional red flags contributing to investigators' suspicions. A local Krispy Kreme employee told investigators that Humphrey had struck up a conversation with her one day, fascinated that she dissected bodies in her human anatomy class. She remembered the discussion because he had asked her if she ever took skin or body parts home to "mess around with it."

University of Florida Police had their own records of incidents with Humphrey. Earlier in the summer, on June 22, he had exchanged hostile words with the driver of a car behind him who had honked angrily due to Humphrey's "very slow" speed. During the altercation, Humphrey threatened the other driver with his knife. That same month, another University police officer had stopped Humphrey for driving erratically. After being pulled over, Humphrey seemed nervous and became upset. When the officer let him go with a warning, Humphrey started driving down the wrong side of the road, so the officer stopped him again and issued a ticket for careless driving.

Witnesses reported seeing Humphrey at a party in Gatorwood at around 10:30 p.m. on Friday night, August 24. Christa Hoyt had also attended that party, which was hosted by the twin sister of Humphrey's ex-girlfriend. Another witness, a maintenance worker at Hawaiian Village, had met Humphrey as he was moving his belongings into an apartment. The worker remembered the encounter because of the anger Humphrey expressed towards his girlfriend, ranting that he wanted to "cut her up and cut her head off."

Around 2:00 a.m. on Saturday, August 25, Humphrey had threatened two UF students with a knife outside the Pi Lambda Phi fraternity house. Shortly afterward, a University Police foot patrol officer saw Humphrey speeding down Fraternity Row in a black Cadillac. When the officer yelled at him to slow down, Humphrey made a U-turn and drove back to the officer to apologize. During their conversation,

Humphrey sweated profusely and mentioned that he wanted to join the military so he could fight in the Middle East. The encounter lasted a few minutes, and then Humphrey drove away.

More recently, on August 27, two officers had responded to the Hawaiian Village apartment complex in connection with Humphrey's grandmother's request that they check on him. Humphrey moved into apartment 131 of Hawaiian Village on August 18 after being asked to move out of Gatorwood by his roommates. He called his grandmother the morning of August 27 complaining that his car had been towed or stolen. When the officers arrived at Humphrey's apartment around 2:00 that afternoon, he seemed disoriented when he answered the door and told the officers that he would be joining the military to help solve the Mideast crisis. He also brought up the student murders and said that whoever killed them must be a "sicko." He eventually asked the University Police to help find his car, which he had lost on campus after parking it near the library. The police subsequently located Humphrey's car, not near the library, but by a dormitory elsewhere on campus.

After speaking with task force detectives and reviewing the case files, FBI profiler Jim Wright declared that the likelihood of Humphrey being the killer "looks very good". The veteran agent pointed to Humphrey's recent appearance at his old high school as evidence of his "losing control of the situation" and seeking out "places where he had a stable time in his life." Wright called the students' murderer a "rare one" who wanted his victims to be found, but who also demonstrated criminal sophistication. He opined that Humphrey "feels superior to the police task force" and that the mutilations to Christa Hoyt's body were probably meant as a message to police. He also warned that the "next stressful thing" in Humphrey's life could "trigger him to start killing again."

Another suspect also surfaced. Polk County police arrested Steven Bates, described as "very muscular with satanic-type tattoos all over his body," for the armed burglary of a white female's residence. His use of a large butcher's knife during the crime piqued task force investigators' interest. During an interview after his arrest, Bates told police about a dream in which he cut off a woman's head, placed it on her nightstand, and then had sex with her body while her head watched. The similarity to Christa Hoyt's murder seemed more than mere coincidence. Bates also admitted that he had been in the Archer Road area, and on the Gatorwood property in particular, on the night of Friday, August 24.

Although Bates was now squarely on the radar, Humphrey remained the top suspect. Negative results on an FDLE fingerprint analysis did not dissuade detectives' belief that Humphrey was the killer, particularly since fortune seemed to smile on the investigative efforts shortly afterward.

Just two hours after their August 30 meeting, task force leaders learned that Humphrey had been arrested earlier that morning. They were elated at the news that their top suspect was in custody and being held in the Brevard County jail.

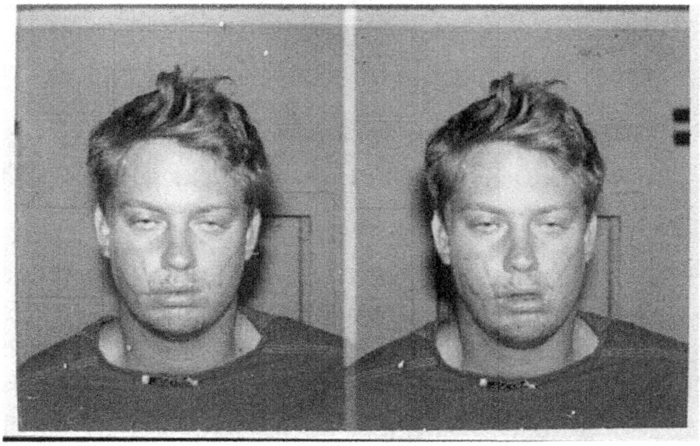

Ed Humphrey's Booking Photos

Chapter 8

May 1990

Shreveport, Louisiana

On May 18, 1990, the convict has a violent feud with his abusive father and nearly kills the elder man. The fight starts when he walks into the kitchen and puts his foot on a bench to tie his shoe. When his father sees him, he yells at him to get his foot off the bench. Instead of obeying, the convict looks at his father and smirks.

"I got my foot on the bench, old man," he snarls. "What are you going to do about it?"

"I'll tell you what I'm going to do about it," his father growls before hurrying to the back of the house.

The convict finishes tying his shoes and starts walking out the door when his father runs into the kitchen with a gun bellowing, "I'll get rid of all of you!" He darts outside as his father chases after him, gun in hand, firing three shots into the air, before storming back into the house and bolting the door behind him. As his father picks up the kitchen phone to make a call, the convict crashes through the door and crouches down by the table in a defensive position.

"You want to shoot somebody," he screams at his father, "you want to kill somebody, kill me, but don't hurt my mom!"

As his father turns toward him firing two more shots, he fires three shots of his own from a .38 pistol he retrieved from the tool shed outside. Two of the bullets hit their target, striking his father in the stomach and right between the eyes. He collapses onto the kitchen floor. Cursing his father, the convict kicks him before fleeing from the house.

Around 10:00 p.m. that night, Steve Clausen and his wife, Louisa Biedenharn, are relaxing in the upstairs bedroom of their Shreveport home. Steve is sitting next to the fireplace on a couch watching television with Louisa lying near him in their bed when he hears her let out a frightened gasp. As Steve looks over at her, he feels the presence of someone behind him. He turns around and sees the convict standing in the double-door entry to the bedroom dressed in camouflage pants, army boots, and a t-shirt with a bandanna around his head. He is holding a gun in his hand.

"You really need to get security lighting," he tells the surprised couple.

Steve and Louisa met him several weeks earlier when they went out for dinner at the Superior Grill in Shreveport. They had been waiting in the lounge area for a table, talking about putting in security lighting around their 30-acre property, when he turned around from where he was seated next to them.

"Excuse me," he said, "I couldn't help but overhear your conversation, and I happen to be in the electrical business. Could I come out sometime and make a bid on the job?"

They talked with him for about thirty minutes that night. He seemed "very honest," "very nice," and "very polite." They agreed for him to come to their home the following week to give an estimate on the electrical work. A few nights after that, he showed up unexpectedly, knocking on their rear window downstairs. After inviting him in, they could not help but notice that he had been drinking. As they talked, he opened up to them and even disclosed that he had served time in jail. He told them that they had been nicer to him than anyone had ever been, including his own family.

And now he stood in front of them with a gun, having broken into their house by prying open the French doors downstairs.

"I'm in big trouble," he blurts out. "I just shot my father! I want all of your money! I need to get out of town."

The surprised couple tries to calm him down.

"I thought you were our friend," Steve tells him.

"I am your friend," the convict replies as tears appear on his cheeks. He motions to a panel on the wall. "Your burglar alarm is going to go off and the security company will be calling. You better give them the right code word because I saw your alarm system and I know how it works."

Moments later, the phone rings. He moves closer to Steve and puts the gun to his head.

"Give them the right code word," he warns.

Steve answers the phone and assures the company that everything is fine, giving them the correct password in the process. After hanging up the phone, Steve tries appealing to their friendship.

"Why don't you put the gun down?" he says. "We don't keep cash in the house. And whatever you did couldn't be so bad that we can't help you get through it."

The convict slowly lowers the gun to his side.

"Hey, man, you don't want to do this. Why don't you just give me the gun and we'll help you however we can. We're your friends. Come on, give me the gun."

After some hesitation, as if unsure about what to do, he hands over the gun. Steve takes it into the next room and unloads it, then returns to the bedroom. But in a true Jekyll and Hyde manner, by the time Steve steps back into the bedroom, the convict has another gun in his hand.

"Where's my gun?" he bellows.

"It's in the other room," Steve replies, surprised by the sudden mood change. "I'll go get it for you," he says defeatedly.

He retrieves the gun and gives it back to the convict, who feels the weight of the gun in his hand.

"Where's the bullets?" he asks.

Steve hands the bullets to him. He hoped that the convict would not notice the lighter weight of the unloaded gun.

"Don't screw around with me," the convict warns. "It wouldn't bother me to kill you two, seeing as how I just killed my father."

Steve and Louisa exchanges nervous glances.

"Sorry, man, I'm just really nervous," Steve tells him. "I've been having these anxiety attacks, and my pills for them are downstairs. Can we go get them?"

The convict agrees and Louisa convinces him to call the hospital to find out whether his father is really dead. Identifying himself as a relative, he learns that his father is in critical condition, but is still alive and his condition is stabilizing.

Obviously relieved, the convict's mood lightens, and Steve and Louisa's nerves are able to relax a little as well. Over the next two hours, his internal struggle manifests in alternating moments of kindness and anger. At times he sobs and puts the guns down on the table, other times he picks the guns back up and becomes belligerent again.

Recalling the encounter years later, Steve will say that "it was like you were talking to two different people. One polite and one very hostile personality."

At one point, the convict tells Steve that he wants a ride to Dallas, Texas.

"I can't drive you to Dallas," Steve replies.

"He's not driving you *anywhere*," Louisa asserts.

The convict looks at Louisa with surprised eyes.

"Okay," he says gently.

After a few moments of silence, Louisa speaks.

"I have some cash in my purse you can have," she says. She walks over to her purse and takes out $30 cash, which she hands to him. Then she gives him some cookies and an apple from the kitchen.

He stands motionless, holding the money and food in his hands, as if stunned to have been given them.

"Well, I better get going," he finally murmurs. He walks out the door, but steps back inside seconds later.

"It sure is cold out there," he says.

Steve walks over to the closet and pulls out a coat.

"Here, take this," he says, handing him the coat.

"Thanks," the convict says as he puts it on. "You know, you're never supposed to leave witnesses," he adds, staring at the couple who have been so kind to him. "Promise me that you're not going to call the police after I leave."

"We promise," Steve assures him, while Louisa nods in agreement.

The convict peers at them. A slight smile appears on his face.

"Sorry about tracking mud on your carpet," he says. "God bless you all."

This time when he walks out the door he does not return.

After leaving Shreveport, he travels through multiple states, committing rapes and robberies along the way. He makes his way to Kansas City, Kansas, by Greyhound bus, where he lives with "some long hair hippies" for about a month. In June 1990, he robs two Kansas City grocery stores and a Taco Bell, and breaks into a home in Roeland Park where he steals the identification card of Michael Kennedy, Jr. along with a .22 handgun. During the June 12 robbery of the Westwood United Superstore in Kansas City, he tells the cashiers, "Thank you, God bless. Please pray for me, I need it." He escapes with over $1,600, then comes back on June 30 to rob the same store again, this time taking over $2,000.

He travels by bus to Boulder, Colorado, where he attempts to rape a blonde woman on a mountain climbing trip. When she resists, he beats her until her face turns bloody. She pleads with him to stop, and for some reason he does. He lets her go and watches as she runs down the mountain screaming hysterically. In Denver, he robs a downtown convenience store with the .22 stolen in Kansas City, then he hitchhikes his way back to Kansas City before heading south again.

Chapter 9

August 1990

Brevard County, Florida

"Innocent 'til proven guilty!" (Edward Humphrey)

At 2:20 a.m. on August 30, 1990, Deputy Doug Hammack of the Brevard County Sheriff's Office responded to 79-year-old Elon Hlavaty's home. As he pulled his patrol car into the driveway, Hammack found Hlavaty waiting on the front porch of her plantation-style house with a swollen and bloodied face. According to the 911 call, Hlavaty's grandson, Edward Humphrey, had attacked her while she sat in the living room. It was the fifth time Hammack had been called to the residence because of Humphrey and his grandmother fighting, but this time the fighting had been more than just verbal argument.

After checking on Hlavaty, Deputy Hammack stepped inside the house. He saw blood spattered on a reclining chair, a nearby coffee table, and the carpet. Out of the corner of his eye, he caught a glimpse of Humphrey bounding up the stairs. Hammock followed in pursuit and placed Humphrey under arrest for aggravated battery.

Hammack led Humphrey outside and secured him in the back of his patrol car. After telling Hammock, "I hit her and I'm sorry," Humphrey began banging his head on the rear window while screaming, "I'm going to kill myself!" over and over again.

Treated at the hospital for a facial fracture and swollen right eye, Hlavaty gave a sworn statement asserting that, shortly after arriving home from Gainesville, Humphrey had screamed at her: "You are going to hell and you're going to die!" Then he tried to choke her and, when she fell out of her chair, he punched her in the face.

When task force leaders learned of Humphrey's arrest, they dispatched nearby FDLE agents Wally Gossett and Dominic Pape to interview Humphrey at Sharpes, the Brevard County Detention Center. During the late-night, rambling interrogation, Humphrey denied any involvement in the Gainesville murders, but at times he referred to himself as "John" and demonstrated some knowledge of the killings.

Humphrey told his interviewers that a man with a "mean edge" had killed the five students and stated that the man, "John," was inside him.

"There's some psychopath running loose," Humphrey's "John" persona said, "and he's not taking any prisoners . . . . I'll tell you exactly who he is. Probably like a Ninja. Probably really thin. Probably like me."

Ed came across as Humphrey's Dr. Jekyll side: "I never killed anyone, man. I never will, man. I swear to God. I never, never, ever – that's just not me, man."

John seemed to be his Mr. Hyde.

"John, who killed them?" the FDLE agent asked.

"I did," Humphrey replied in his John persona. When asked if he used a weapon in the killings, John replied, "Just a knife." He went on to describe some of the knife wounds and said the victims "didn't know what was hitting them."

In addition to answering the agents' questions, Humphrey voluntarily provided head and pubic hair samples and gave blood samples as well.

That evening, Gainesville Police Department investigators arrived in the Melbourne Beach area to search a wooded location on South Highway A1A where Humphrey had been spotted walking out of the woods. With the help of Palm Beach Sheriff's deputies and K-9 units, they found a pair of ladies' panties in the woods, but their efforts revealed nothing else of potential evidentiary value. A separate search using metal detectors in a shallow creek near

Humphrey's apartment in Gainesville turned up nothing except coat hangers and beer cans.

Meanwhile, a hastily obtained search warrant for Steven Bates's house resulted in the seizure of satanic writings, pornographic material, white medical tape, bloodied clothing, drawings of females in positions similar to those of the posed murder victims, Dawn dishwashing detergent, knives, and a book on Jack the Ripper. Investigators also confirmed that Bates had been in Gainesville from Thursday, August 23 through Monday, August 27, placing him there squarely within the time frame of the killings.

Gainesville Police Chief Wayland Clifton applauded the progress of the investigation.

"With each passing hour, we feel more confident that we will be able to bring this case to successful closure," he announced, adding that detectives were "looking very closely at many persons that have been acting very oddly."

~~~~~

As Humphrey lingered in a Melbourne jail, task force investigators began compiling a chronology of his past. The youngest of four children to George and Elna Humphrey, Edward was born in Winchester, Massachusetts, on October 5, 1971. He attended elementary school in Great Falls, Virginia, and then moved to the Space Coast town of Indialantic, Florida, south of Cape Canaveral and near Melbourne Beach. After the move to Florida, Humphrey's father, a Harvard Business School graduate and former bank executive, started a high-tech company, International Technology Corporation, and worked long hours away from home to get it up and running. Despite his father's frequent absences, Humphrey did well in school and extracurricular activities, including Boy Scouts where he attained the highest rank of Eagle Scout. A member of the Student Council, Key Club, and Spanish Club, he also surfed and played soccer and football. Things changed in 1987 when his parents went through a bitter divorce that deeply affected
~~~~~

him. He sank into a depression and his grades and behavior steadily deteriorated. Friends noticed that his personality drastically changed after a long bout with mononucleosis when he was 16.

"He started thinking Satan was after him," recalled his friend Erik Bedesem. "He wore gardening gloves and a tie as a sash to repel Satan."

Soon afterward, Humphrey began suffering extreme mood changes and experiencing other symptoms of manic-depression, culminating in an episode in 1988 when he jumped out of his brother's car while it was traveling 60 miles per hour.

He graduated from Melbourne High School in the spring of 1989. A few months later, he fell asleep while driving on South Patrick Drive. His Mercury Marquis ran off the road and slammed into a concrete utility pole. Upon impact, Humphrey smashed into the windshield, shattering the glass and badly slicing his face. He also suffered a collapsed lung and a compound fracture of his right leg so severe that a steel rod had to be implanted, confining him to the hospital for three weeks and then crutches for months after his discharge.

Following a semester at Brevard Community College, Humphrey applied to UF and was accepted for the six-week summer term. He went to Gainesville in June 1990 and lived in one of the campus dormitories while taking classes. He planned on continuing his studies there in the fall.

In July, police ejected Humphrey from an Indialantic surf shop after he threatened several customers by telling them that he would cut their hearts out. On August 5, his grandmother called the police to report that he was "high" on drugs, and a neighbor reported hearing him shouting that he would kill his grandparents. The next day, at Patrick Air Force Base near Cocoa Beach, a military police officer encountered Humphrey running in circles, talking to himself, and chewing on a beer can. He told the officer that he wanted to join the military so that he could "hang people up and gut them like deer." Military police found two knives with 6-inch blades under the seat of his car. They took him into custody but released him three hours later to his mother.

A couple of weeks later in Gainesville, Humphrey threatened two members of Pi Lambda Phi fraternity with a knife by making a sawing motion across his throat. His encounters with police escalated until the August 30 arrest for assaulting his grandmother. Diagnosed in high school as manic depressive, Humphrey had been prescribed lithium to treat his mental illness, but in the weeks leading up to his arrest, he stopped taking his medication.

Instead of returning to Gainesville to continue taking classes, he was arrested for battery and put in solitary confinement in a cell 10 feet wide by 10 feet long, let out in leg chains and handcuffs once a week to visit his lawyer and twice a week to shower.

Shackled and chained with deputies holding both of his arms, Humphrey grinned at TV cameras during his August 30 arraignment on the battery charge arising from the alleged assault of his grandmother. He repeatedly crossed himself as if warding away evil spirits. After Judge Kerry Evander found probable cause to hold Humphrey for trial, Humphrey spoke up.

"Can I say something?" he asked the judge.

"You should ask your attorney," the judge advised, motioning to public defender J.R. Russo.

"Innocent till proven guilty!" Humphrey blurted out before Russo could react.

Elon Hlavaty grimly watched the proceedings from the courtroom gallery, her face bruised and her right eye swollen shut. Asked if Humphrey caused her injury, Hlavaty had a curt response.

"I hit that on the fireplace," she sneered. "Shut up."

Detectives interviewed Humphrey's brother, who told them that Humphrey's personality had changed in recent months and had been getting worse the last few weeks. Many other witnesses gave statements similar to that of a convenience store clerk at a location Humphrey frequented, who said that he "gave everybody the creeps." However, not everyone had bad things to say about him. Humphrey's former history teacher said he had been a model student prior to his car accident.

"I'd have a taken a room full of students like him," Bill Thomas unequivocally asserted.

Witnesses and receipts established that Humphrey had left Gainesville the afternoon of August 25 and purchased gas in Titusville at 8:48 p.m. His brother saw him asleep in bed in his mother's Indialantic home at 10:00 a.m. on August 26, and later saw him leave to go back to Gainesville at 8:00 p.m. that night. Humphrey's friend, Mark Vincutonis, claimed that Humphrey stopped by to visit him and have dinner in Orlando from 9:30 to 11:30 p.m., and a credit card receipt placed Humphrey at a Winter Park gas station the night of the 26th at 11:54 p.m.

Although his bond had initially been set at $10,250 after his arrest, Brevard County prosecutors succeeded in convincing the court to raise the bond to $1 million, an amount 100 to 200 times the normal bond for an assault charge like Humphrey's.

Brevard County Public Defender J.R. Russo could barely believe how high the judge set his teenaged client's bond. Outraged by the enormity of the number, he wasted no time speaking out against it, despite the fact that the effort was doomed from the start.

"Are we holding a citizen just because he fits a certain mental psychological profile, or do they have specific evidence which justifies a million-dollar bond?" Russo demanded.

Assistant State Attorney Michael Hunt confirmed that the drastically increased bond was due to outside influences and unusual circumstances.

"State investigators talked to us," he acknowledged. "Gainesville is a factor. I'm not saying he's the killer, but the fact is that some things have surfaced in that investigation that convince us he is a serious danger to the community."

Brevard State Attorney Norm Wolfinger admitted the same.

"Yes, this is a Gainesville issue," Wolfinger affirmed. "We have to look at all of the facts. We're not going to hide our heads in the sand."

Following a 90-minute hearing, Circuit Judge Martin Budnick refused to reduce Humphrey's bail amount.

> It's obvious to the court that the only charge on which Mr. Humphrey is being held is the aggravated battery upon his grandmother, and certainly, the bond should be established on that charge. However, if I were to lower it, I'm afraid I would do a disservice to the defendant, the family, and the community. I see before me what appears to be a very disturbed individual. I'm not confident or comfortable that Mr. Humphrey is in control of himself. I see a great deal of acting out neurotic or psychotic behavior and that has to concern me. I feel at this point he may be a danger to the community.

~~~~~
~~~~~

On Friday, August 31, family and friends gathered across Florida to remember the five young lives brutally ended by their still unknown killer. At St. David's Episcopal Church in Jacksonville, hundreds of people honored Christi Powell.

"The thing I remember most about her was her bubbly personality and her great hugs," her former youth minister, Darrell Cope, recalled fondly.

First Baptist Church in Pompano Beach offered comfort to the over 1,000 mourners that Sonja Larson was "probably in glory already, taking care of children. That was her plan," and promising that her killer would "face a stronger judge than I."

Near Gainesville, close to 500 people packed the auditorium at Newberry High School to share memories of Christa Hoyt, and in Miami, a similar crowd gathered to mourn Tracy Paules and Manny Taboada. Tracy lay in a silver-colored coffin in Van Orsdel Chapel in Coral Gables, wearing the same blue satin gown she had worn when she was named homecoming queen at American High School.

"She was a really good friend, just full of life," said Tony Miller, one of the attendees. "She always had a smile. This is just a senseless thing. It's such a waste."

At Manny's service in Hialeah, most of his high school classmates came to pay their respects.

"A lot of these people haven't seen each other in six years," said Fred Harvey, Manny's teammate on the American High School football team. "Only somebody like Manny could bring so many people back. They're really hurting. We expected to have our whole lives ahead of us."

Much earlier that morning, during the dark, after-midnight hours, Gainesville police spotted a man walking along SW 20th Avenue near the three murder scenes. Clad in camouflage pants, the man darted away when he noticed the police approaching. They pursued him through the Mill

Run Apartments complex and into a nearby woods before losing sight of him. Dozens of officers and police dogs searched the woods to no avail. Even a police helicopter failed to find him.

~~~~~

As their August 31 meeting concluded, task force leaders advised team members that if the investigation was not completed by the following weekend, many of them staying in area hotels would have to find other accommodations. The University of Florida had a home football game scheduled against Oklahoma State on Saturday, September 8. With the return of the Gators' Heisman Trophy-winning quarterback, Steve Spurrier, to his alma mater as its new head football coach, Gator Nation buzzed with excitement about his inaugural season. Hotels throughout the Gainesville area had been booked well in advance for the weekend. Even the prospect of a serial killer on the loose would not deter die-hard alumni who bled orange and blue from making their way to UF's home stadium, popularly known as the Swamp. That Saturday, an enthusiastic crowd would pack the Swamp to watch their beloved Gators pummel OSU 50 to 7.

Fortunately, the need for long-term lodging of task force members looked less and less likely. Confident that they had identified the killer, Gainesville law enforcement began hinting that an arrest could soon be coming.

"Our investigation is going very well, and we're very encouraged," Lt. Sadie Darnell, Gainesville Police Department spokesman, announced at a news conference in early September.

Likewise, Lt. Spencer Mann, spokesman for the Sheriff's Office, acknowledged that the investigation had reached a critical point, although arrest warrants had not yet been sought.
~~~~~

Even Captain Ward, co-Chief of the task force, hinted that an arrest could be coming sooner rather than later.

"We just need a few breaks," Ward said. "We're very close."

Chapter 10

Summer 1990

Florida

By July 17, 1990, the fugitive finds his way to Tallahassee, Florida. Using the alias, Michael Kennedy, Jr., he checks into the Travel Lodge on West Tennessee Street. The next day, he buys a Marine Ka-Bar fighting knife at the Army-Navy store near the bus station in Tallahassee.

On July 22, he takes a bus to Sarasota, Florida, where he checks into the Cabana Inn hotel using the stolen identity of Michael Kennedy, Jr. While there, he records songs on a portable tape player he previously stole, and he starts a “farewell” message to his family, the rest of which he will record in August. During his time in Sarasota, he befriends a salesman at Burdine’s department store, and the two go to several area restaurants and strip clubs together. He also dates a woman he meets at the Cabana Inn bar. When his money starts running low on August 8, he moves from the Cabana Inn to the Sunnyside Inn, a cheaper motel across the street. He stays there for three nights, then leaves town.

On August 18, he steps off a bus in Gainesville. Still using the name Michael Kennedy, he checks into the University Inn on 13th Street, paying cash to rent Room 104. He spends the next few days scoping out the area. He marvels that there are so many attractive young brunette women around.

On August 23, he checks out of the hotel and makes a campsite in a clearing in the woods on the eastern side of SW 34th Street, approximately 250 yards from the road at the corner of Archer Road. At the center of the camp, he puts up a small tent he purchased at a Gainesville Walmart. The same day, he sees *Exorcist III* at the Litchfield Theater. The movie features a decapitation and a killer possessed by a bloodthirsty demon named Gemini. Gemini also happens to be his astrological sign.

Later that night, a security guard stumbles across the fugitive as he stands on a large bucket peeping into the second story window of an apartment. When the guard asks him what he is doing, the fugitive confuses him by replying in an accusatory tone, “I saw what you did”. He calmly walks past the bewildered guard and disappears into the dark woods.

Just before noon on August 27, shirtless but wearing a brown ski mask, he storms into the First Union Bank on SW Archer Road, just down the street from Christa Hoyt’s apartment.

“This is a robbery! Put your hands up!” he shouts while waving a metallic-blue handgun. “No one will be hurt if you all cooperate!”

Carrying a dark-colored duffel bag across his shoulders, he jumps over the counter and smashes the security camera with the gun. He orders the bank tellers to fill the bag with money.

“You ladies come open up these drawers!” he yells to the nearest tellers. “Give me the money out of these drawers!”

As the tellers comply, he glances toward the entrance.

“I see what you’re doing, signaling someone!” he bellows to a customer in the lobby near the front door. “Don’t do that! Don’t move!” he screams, pointing the gun at her.

Turning back to the bank tellers, he eyes them suspiciously.

“There better not be any dye packs in there!” he warns as the tellers continue stuffing money into his bag.

After closing the bag of money, he strides toward the door.

“Don’t anyone move!” he snarls. “Don’t do anything!

As he hurries out the door, he sneers at them in a sarcastic tone. “Have a nice fucking day!”

Seconds later, not fifty yards from the bank, red dye packs concealed within the stolen money explode causing red smoke to billow out of the top of the bag. As he continues running across the parking lot toward the Dollar General store, witnesses see him removing the ski mask from his face.

~~~~~

Around 1:00 a.m. the next morning, Officer Tim Merrill notices two men, one white and one black, walking north on S.W. 34th Street. He watches as they walk into a wooded area approximately half a mile from the First Union Bank on SW Archer Road. Aware of the recent bank robbery, Officer Merrill calls for back-up and follows the two men into the woods. When Merrill orders them to stop, the black male complies, but the white male sprints deeper into the woods. Merrill chases the white male a few hundred yards through the darkness until he loses sight of him in denser tree cover.

After being detained, the black male, 34-year-old Tony Danzy, tells the officers that he recently met “Mike,” the white male who ran away, at Taco Bell. Mike said that he lived in a campsite in the woods and had money there that he was saving to go to Kansas City. Danzy had given Mike a ride across town for a promised payment of $10.00 when they reached Mike’s tent.

A K-9 police dog tracks Mike’s scent to a campsite about 300 feet into the woods. Although no one is there, police find a large amount of dye-stained money under a
~~~~~

raincoat on the ground and inside a tote bag in a small tent. The officers also find a blue steel Taurus 9 mm handgun, various jewelry, a brown-colored ski mask, gloves, and a small cassette player with a tape. Subsequent assistance from the FBI will reveal that the handgun originally belonged to Robert Ford of Sarasota, who sold it to a man named "Michael," a drifter staying at the Cubana Inn on the Tamiami Trail, earlier in the summer.

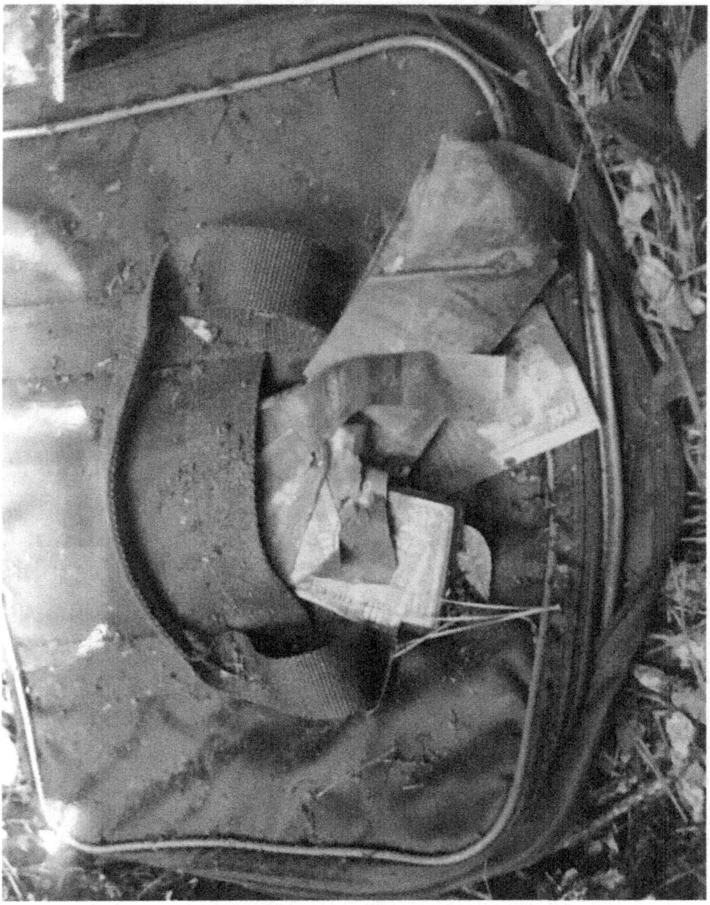

Robbery money with exploding red dye

Gun used in Bank Robbery

On the afternoon of August 30, University of Florida engineering student Christopher Osborne returns to his home on NW 12th Street and finds the front door unlocked and leaning open. Someone had broken into his house by removing a screen and forcing open a bedroom window. The thief had apparently made himself at home by eating cookies and Quaker instant oatmeal and watching a Playboy videotape. The burglar left the TV on and dirty dishes in the sink before driving away in Osborne's car, a tan 1978 Buick Regal.

Chapter 11

1989-1990

Shreveport, Louisiana

"You can't make sense out of something that is senseless"

(Karen Martinez, friend of Julie Grissom)

On September 1, 1990, FDLE agent Don Maines travelled to Shreveport, Louisiana, to meet with Sgt. Don Ashley of the Shreveport Police Department. Maines made the trip to investigate similarities between the five student slayings in Gainesville and a triple homicide that had occurred the prior year in Shreveport.

The Grissom Triple Homicide (November 1989)

When 8-year-old Sean Grissom did not show up for school at Turner Elementary on Monday, November 6, 1989, and no one could reach his grandfather, William Grissom, family members became concerned. Sean's mother called the police that Monday morning after her repeated phone calls to the Grissom house went unanswered. Police then contacted neighbors to request that they check to see if the house was locked.

The elder Grissom, a gregarious 55-year-old known as Tom to his friends, was well-liked in the affluent Southern Hills development, a Shreveport neighborhood that he had lived in for nearly twenty years. At the behest of Shreveport police, shortly before 8:45 a.m., friend and neighbor, Bob Coyles, walked to Tom Grissom's brown-brick, three-bedroom house at 2011 Beth Lane to make sure everything was okay. When he arrived at the front door, the house was eerily quiet. Coyles walked to the side of the house and cracked the laundry room door open. He froze in horror, staring at a body sprawled on the floor in blood-soaked clothes. Terrified, he slammed the door shut and sprinted home to call the police.

After police arrived they confirmed the dreaded news. It was Tom Grissom's body in the laundry room. He had suffered multiple stab wounds to his chest. Venturing further into the house, they found Sean Grissom face down in the family room near his Nintendo videogame and Halloween candy. The young boy had been killed by a single stab wound that passed through his back and exited his chest. Two murders were bad enough, but that was not the extent of the killings. In the bedroom, police discovered a third body. It was 24-year-old Julie Grissom. Lying on her back, nude with bite marks covering her breasts, Julie had been repeatedly slashed and stabbed in the back. Her body was posed on the bed in a sexually suggestive manner, her legs spread apart, her arms stretched upward, and her hair fanned out around her head.

~~~~~

Less than 48 hours earlier, around 6:00 p.m. on Saturday, November 4, Tom Grissom had busied himself cooking beef on the propane grill in his backyard. He was happy to have guests for the weekend, having picked up his grandson from his son's house earlier that day. While Tom grilled, Sean Grissom watched television in the den, excited about spending the weekend with his grandfather and aunt as part of his eighth birthday celebration. Neighbors last saw Tom and Sean around 5:20 p.m. that evening when they were outside together in the yard. Not long afterward, Julie pulled into the driveway and hurried into the house. An attractive young woman with sandy-brown hair and green eyes, Julie had just returned home from her job as a Liz Claiborne sales clerk at Dillard's department store in Shreveport's South Park Mall. After taking classes at Louisiana State University for several years in Baton Rouge, she had come back to Shreveport to help out her dad and save money while finishing school.
~~~~~

Within minutes of Julie's arrival home from work, an unseen intruder snuck into the house through an unlocked door, carrying a knife and wielding malice in his heart.

~~~~~

The pine-tree dotted Shreveport neighborhood reacted with shock and disbelief to the news of the triple homicide.

"I just can't understand it," said neighbor Sally Stephenson. "Tom was always nice, would always wave. I can't imagine anyone doing this to them."

"It's a nightmare," Bob Coyles echoed. He and Tom had been close and frequently went on fishing trips together. "We were good neighbors and good friends," he said sadly. "You couldn't ask for a nicer neighbor."

The whole thing seemed surreal, unbelievable, simply unimaginable.

"You just don't think about something like this happening in your neighborhood," Coyle explained. "It's always across town or somewhere else. It's not supposed to happen next door."

In recent months, Tom had looked forward to his approaching retirement as section chief for a business communications systems department at AT & T. He had been June Davis's supervisor.

"He was one of the finest men I've ever known," Davis said. "He always smiled."

Karen Martinez, one of Julie Grissom's closest friends, saw her at Dillard's just a few hours before the murders. The two had been friends since they were five years old. They grew up in the same quiet neighborhood of three-bedroom, two-bath homes. They carpooled to school together and joined the dance team at Southwood High School where their classmates elected Julie to the
~~~~~

homecoming court. Karen had thought so highly of Julie that she borrowed Julie's dress to wear to her own senior prom. Now her life-long friend was gone.

"You can't make sense out of something that is senseless," Martinez sighed, "although you try."

Shreveport attorney Hal Carter, a former boyfriend of Julie's, struggled to maintain his composure as he watched police coming and going from the Grissom home.

"If ever I've known someone who deserves to be in heaven, Julie does, and her dad," he exclaimed. He and Julie had met at South Park Mall the previous year when he stopped in to shop for luggage.

"How could someone do something so awful to people so sweet, gentle and kind?" he asked no one in particular, needing to give voice to his distraught thoughts. "It's so awful – just senseless. It's not fair."

Shreveport detectives had no suspects in mind as they tried to determine a motive for the murders.

"It doesn't appear to have been a robbery," said Lt. Gary Pittman of the Shreveport Police Department. His men had already canvassed the entire neighborhood. "So far no one recalls anything out of the ordinary. Whether a dog barked or whatever, nobody remembers. But then, nobody was expecting anything to happen."

Several days into the investigation, Lt. Pittman became convinced that the Grissoms knew their killer. The absence of any signs of forced entry and the elimination of robbery as the perpetrator's motivation "indicated closeness to the family."

~~~~~

On November 9, over 400 mourners attended Tom and Julie Grissom's funeral at Rose-Neath Funeral Home in Shreveport. Family, friends, and neighbors quietly filled the
~~~~~

chapel's pews and aisles. When the funeral home chapel reached full capacity, several dozen people had to view the service from the foyer.

"Their deaths are tragic," Reverend Paul Hutzler told the somber crowd, "but we must have faith in God. We who are believers know we'll see our departed loved ones in heaven one day."

Following the service, a long line of mourners passed in front of the side-by-side caskets, his blue, hers pinkish-white. Many of those in the procession paused briefly to pay their respects. Father and daughter were buried two days later at Washington Park East Cemetery in Cumberland, Indiana, where they had lived before moving to Louisiana. Sean Grissom's funeral took place the day after his grandfather and aunt's. At the Boone Funeral Home service in Bossier City, a family friend offered a consoling thought.

"God has a special love for children," she said.

On Friday, November 10, Shreveport police named Hal Carter as a suspect in the Grissom murders. Detectives interviewed him at his office and examined a Delta Airlines ticket he produced to support the alibi that he was in Atlanta at the time of the murders.

"I didn't kill her," Carter insisted of his former girlfriend, Julie. To illustrate how deeply her death had affected him, Carter pointed out that since her murder, he had needed tranquilizers to help him sleep.

A week later, Carter announced at a news conference that the police had cleared him as a suspect after interviewing four people in Atlanta to corroborate his alibi.

"Police have verified those witnesses and documentation," he asserted. "They now know I was in Atlanta."

Strangely, police spokeswoman Cindy Chadwick stopped short of exonerating Carter. "We haven't eliminated anyone as a suspect," she said flatly.

"I feel like police generate this idea that Hal Carter is a murderer," an indignant Carter proclaimed. "They have the obligation and should, to at least say publicly, 'Look, we checked out where he was and Hal Carter was in Atlanta, Georgia, over the weekend of the Grissom murders'. The reality is there is a triple murderer out there and he is not Hal Carter."

As more weeks passed, Shreveport police acknowledged that the likelihood of an arrest in the case was becoming less and less likely. Although they had nothing significant to go on, they vowed to keep following up leads until the killer was found.

"The first 72 hours are crucial," admitted Captain John Snell. "After the first 72 hours, the investigation becomes more difficult. But we've got to get this guy, this person, for this vicious crime. We owe it to ourselves. We owe it to the community and we owe it to the victims."

During its December 20 fall commencement ceremony, Louisiana State University Shreveport awarded Julie Grissom a posthumous degree in marketing.

"She was just so full of life," said childhood friend Karen Kotarski. "She had so much to give, so much potential. It wasn't fair to have all this taken away from her."

Another long-time friend echoed those sentiments.

"She was the sweetest person I ever met in my life," said Nancy Rak. "She was just a good person who was down to earth. She didn't deserve what happened to her."

~~~~~

On March 8, 1990, Shreveport police effectively acknowledged that the Grissom investigation had reached a
~~~~~

dead end. The only detective still working on the case full-time was removed and reassigned to other cases.

"We have other unsolved homicides and we owe each and every one of them all that we can give them," Lt. Gary Pittman explained. "The progress of the Grissom investigation at this time is that we have no suspects," he admitted. Then he quickly added, "I don't have any doubt we'll get the killer of the Grissoms. To tell you a date, I don't know."

The decision to shift the unsolved triple murder to inactive status disappointed the Grissom family. Tom Grissom's sister-in-law, Doris, summed up the family's frustration with the status of the investigation.

"It bothers me knowing the killer is still out there. I guess he'll probably have to kill someone else before they get him."

Chapter 12

September 1990

Tampa, Florida

After leaving Gainesville, the convict makes his way to Tampa. Around 7:45 p.m. on September 2, 1990, wearing a t-shirt, shorts, and a brown ski mask, he walks into a Save N Pack grocery store at the corner of Nebraska and Fowler Avenue. He tosses paper bags at the cashiers and orders them to fill the bags with money. Hillsborough County Sheriff's deputies eating at a nearby restaurant respond to the store in time to intercept him as he races out with $3,000 and jumps into a Buick Regal. As he starts the engine, two deputies step in front of the car with their guns drawn. He tries to get away by putting the vehicle in reverse, but only manages to smash into the alley and wedge the car there.

"Good for you, asshole!" someone yells from a group of onlookers.

A female deputy strides toward him from behind, weapon aimed at his head, and orders him to get out of the car. Instead, he points his gun at her.

"Lady, I don't want to shoot you," he warns.

After a brief stand-off, the deputy backs around the corner of the building with her gun still drawn. He yanks the gear into drive, floors the gas pedal, and speeds forward as the deputies repeatedly fire at him, shattering the windshield and riddling the car with bullets. In all, they fire 19 shots at the car, hitting it 17 times. Remarkably, not one of the bullets strikes him. Police find the car abandoned several blocks away from the shootout, smoke still wafting from under the hood.

After fleeing through some woods near the abandoned car, scaling a chain-link fence, and sprinting across the highway, the fugitive dashes into a residential area. Spying a suitable target, he breaks into a residence on North Orleans Street at 9:20 p.m. by removing the sliding glass door. He uses the absent resident's phone to place long distance calls to his mother and former girlfriend, Bunnie Mills, then leaves. He breaks into another house nearby whose owners are out of town for Labor Day Weekend, but he soon departs after finding nothing of value. He pedals out of the neighborhood on a 10-speed bike he steals from the back porch and spends the night in a house still under construction.

On September 4, he walks up to Margaret Sanders, a free-lance artist, sitting on a park bench in front of Lowry Park Zoo in Tampa.

"You look like you could use a friend," the fugitive smiles as he stands beside her. "Let me buy you a root beer."

Although surprised, Sanders cannot resist smiling back and accepting his offer. He seems so genuinely friendly and good-natured. She shows him some of the sketches she has completed.

"You're really good," he says. "Could you do one of me?"

Impressed with the finished product, he pays her $100 cash for the portrait and asks her to mail it to him at an address in Dallas, Texas. After learning that he has no place to stay, she invites him to spend the night at her place. They ride the bus to her apartment, and that night they watch *Good Morning Vietnam* on TV while eating Chinese food. He sleeps on her sofa while she sleeps in her bed. Before he leaves the next morning, she gives him written directions for how to find her apartment again.

During the predawn hours the morning of September 7, he breaks into Ray and Patricia Rio's unit in the River Garden Apartments at Tampa Bay Boulevard and Armenia

Avenue in Tampa. With the Rios and their 16-year-old son asleep upstairs, he pries open a glass door downstairs with a screwdriver. While in the apartment, he eats a banana, steals two Timex watches, and takes car keys from the coffee table. Before leaving, he moves a dining room chair over to the bottom of the stairway so it will be the first thing the Rios see when they come downstairs in the morning. He also places a banana peel on the chair. He makes his way to the parking lot and tries out the keys until he finds a fit: a 1983 silver Ford Mustang. He starts the engine and drives away.

Later that day just before 1:00 p.m., he strolls into a Winn-Dixie supermarket on SW College Road in Ocala. He is wearing a fisherman's hat, Bermuda shorts, deck shoes, and sunglasses. He walks up to the nearest cashier and flashes a .38 revolver.

"This is a robbery. Get your money out!" he commands her.

As the nervous cashier complies, he glances into the bag. He gives a slight smile and says, "Bless you," before running out of the store with over $2,000 cash. He jumps into the driver's seat of a silver Mustang, its engine already running. The car darts out of the parking lot, its tires screeching as he turns east on State Road 200 toward downtown Ocala.

In response to a Winn-Dixie employee's 911 call, a swarm of Ocala police quickly converge on the area. Since it happens to be a training day for the police department, twice the number of patrol units are on the streets. The fugitive does not get far before hearing sirens behind him. At first the sirens sound faint and seem distant, but they soon grow louder as a handful of police cruisers appear in hot pursuit. After leading the police on a high-speed chase, he crashes into a car sitting at a stoplight at the intersection of 5th Avenue and SW 10th Street.

The fugitive jumps out of the demolished car and sprints across a parking lot as police squeal to a stop by the abandoned get-away vehicle. He dashes through the door of an office building and down its lobby, startling a worker at his desk, and runs out the back door. He comes to a grass covered lot and stops. With police surrounding him on all sides, he raises his hands and surrenders.

"Boy, you guys are good," the wide-eyed fugitive says as he is handcuffed and taken into custody. "You guys are really good."

Later, the "chatty" armed robbery suspect sits in an Ocala Police Department interrogation room about 30 miles south of Gainesville. He surprises Sergeant Greg Graham of Ocala's Criminal Investigation Division by freely admitting to the robbery.

*****

Many years later, the suspect will speak from prison to a law enforcement class at the FBI's training academy in Quantico, Virginia.

"Going to Ocala was the worst thing I could have done," he tells the class, still amazed about the swarm of law enforcement that had so quickly surrounded him. "There were more police cars there than I'd ever seen in one place before in my life."

Chapter 13

September 1990

Gainesville, Florida

"The worst thing that could happen would be for the police to make an arrest and then find out it's the wrong man." (Liz Jones, Department of Human Services)

Just before midnight in early September 1990, Adam Tritt stopped his scooter at a graffiti-laden concrete wall on Southwest 34th Street in Gainesville. Originally built to hold back dirt and prevent erosion from the University of Florida golf course, the 1,100-foot-long wall had become a place for students and others in the community to spray or sketch any messages that came to mind, from the trivial to the important, whatever warranted expression. Now everyone in the community knew it simply as "the wall."

Tritt, a teacher at City College, with help from his friend Paul Chase, toted $11.25 worth of paint, rollers, and brushes they had bought at Walmart to one of the wall's concrete panels. Tritt and Chase worked in the dark for nearly two hours, ducking out of sight whenever a car passed by on 34th Street, always on the lookout for police since writing on the wall technically constituted a misdemeanor offense. When the two men finished, they left behind a memorial to the five slain students: the names *Sonja Larson, Christina Powell, Christa Hoyt, Manuel Taboada, Tracy Paules* painted prominently on a large panel of the wall and prefaced by one powerful word: *REMEMBER.*

~~~~~

By September 2, 1990, Edward Humphrey's name and booking photo from his Brevard County arrest began
~~~~~

appearing in newspaper articles and TV news reports as far away as California identifying him as a suspect in the Gainesville slayings. Yet, Gainesville police publicly denied that Humphrey was their prime suspect and began backtracking from their previous confident assertions.

"There are several suspects we are considering at this time," Lt. Sadie Darnell insisted on behalf of the Gainesville Police Department.

"To say we have a suspect that is about to be arrested would be very premature," echoed Lt. Spencer Mann of the Sheriff's Office. "We do not have a timetable on an arrest, warrants, or fruition of this case."

Indeed, while devoting the bulk of its resources to Humphrey, the task force continued following up other leads in the case, which now numbered over 1,500. Detectives traveled to Alabama, California, Louisiana, Mississippi, Montana, Nevada, New York, Oregon, and Tennessee in pursuit of leads. The Grissom triple homicide in Louisiana seemed especially worthy of further investigation. Similarities between the Grissom murders and the Gainesville homicides, including that both involved victims with multiple stab wounds and crime scenes with few clues left behind, jumped out at task force member Don Maines. However, Shreveport homicide detective Lt. Gary Pittman, who compared notes with Maines, discounted the similarities.

"There are the stabbings that are similar," Pittman acknowledged, "but based on the information we have, we don't feel they are related."

In Baton Rouge, state police helped with another Louisiana lead by locating a resident who had shared a ride with Humphrey during a trip from Florida to Kansas earlier in the year. Florida investigators wanted to see whether any crimes could be linked to the trip, but like the Shreveport lead, nothing appeared sufficiently pertinent to connect to the Gainesville murders.

Back in Gainesville, an expert crime scene analyst from Mississippi spent three or four hours at each of the three crime scenes using a newly invented ultraviolet imaging system to search for fingerprints. The results of the search left him frustrated.

"I thought I'd seen everything. I've never been associated with a crime scene that had so many violent attacks and so little evidence left behind," said Michael West. "This is not your average criminal. He's very methodical and very neat. He doesn't leave any traces of his presence in the crime scenes."

Gainesville Police Captain Richard Ward, one of three task force leaders, believed that the killer intended to taunt the police by the way he arranged the crime scenes. Another of the task force leaders, J.O. Jackson of the Florida Department of Law Enforcement, agreed.

"He set up a stage for us," Jackson explained, "and when we walked in, we saw the play he had set up for us."

On September 7, forensic anthropologist William Maples joined the task force for a meeting to discuss the weapon used in the five Gainesville murders. Maples had attended the autopsies conducted by Dr. Hamilton and had seen the type and extent of injuries inflicted on the victims. He noted in particular that the hilt of a "large knife" had "left an imprint on one victim's back, and the point exited her chest on the opposite side, a distance of eight inches, during which the knife was fully sheathed, its entire length buried in the unfortunate girl's body."

Based on his initial analysis, Dr. Maples believed the weapon to be a knife with a 7- to 8-inch blade and a "sharp, smooth, non-serrated cutting edge," and it would be a "sturdy knife, like a military weapon." During his subsequent meeting with task force investigators, Maples was asked whether the murder weapon could be a Marine Corps fighting knife, commonly known as a Ka-Bar. Maples opined that it “very well might,” an opinion he later confirmed by visiting a local knife shop and examining a Ka-Bar up close.

~~~~~

Ka-Bar knives trace their origin to 1923 when the manufacturer received a testimonial letter from a fur trapper. The trapper wrote that while trapping, his rifle jammed, leaving him with only his knife to kill a wounded bear that had attacked him. He thanked the company for making the quality knife that helped him kill a bear, but all that was legible in the letter was “K a bar”. The manufacturer liked the name and subsequently designed a new fighting knife for the United State Marine Corps during World War II, something stronger and more durable than what the Marines had been using. The Army, Navy, and Coast Guard soon adopted the Ka-Bar knife as well. It became the knife of choice for causing maximum damage to another living being.

~~~~~

After the Labor Day holiday, the flood of students who had abandoned classes in mass panic slowly began to trickle back to campus. While welcoming their return, school officials and police warned that the killer could still be at large in the Gainesville area. Although much of the public felt reassured by the fact that Edward Humphrey was in custody, some around campus cautioned not to rush to judgment.

“I think everyone wants to think Humphrey is the guy, but I just don’t believe it,” said Angela Smart, a senior majoring in psychology. “After Ted Bundy, the people of Florida grew up a little bit. We know now that not everyone who does this sort of thing is a street thug kind of person.”

Liz Jones, county director for the Department of Human Services, felt similarly.

“There’s still a clamoring to do it fast, but there’s also an equal clamoring to do it right,” she said. “The worst thing that could happen would be for the police to make an arrest and then find out it's the wrong man."

On September 6, task force members oversaw a search of Humphrey's Hawaiian Village apartment. Behind a water heater in a bedroom closet, they found a large military style knife and a map showing a small pond along with the handwritten notation of a star and several "x" symbols.

A search warrant affidavit filed by FDLE agent A.L. Strope asserted that investigators had reason to believe that Humphrey was present when Christi Powell and Sonja Larson were murdered and that a "probability" existed that he was present at the time of Christa Hoyt's murder as well. The affidavit, filed in support of a search of Humphrey's 1979 Cadillac, contended that Humphrey had made statements during questioning on August 30 "implicating himself" and "placing him in the area of the homicides."

Amidst the national media coverage of the case, Cox News Services interviewed popular true crime author Ann Rule, who was closely following the case.

Q: Is Humphrey guilty?

Rule: I don't think so. He's too young. I don't think he's sophisticated enough. They don't get to be serial killers if they're stupid.

Q. Who would mutilate and kill five people? And why?

Rule: A sadistic psychopath. This case resembles Bundy's. The killer is saying, "Look what I did." They want to show the ultimate power they have. They are addicted to murder. Like Bundy, this killer is out of control.

As Humphrey awaited trial in a medical isolation cell at the Brevard County Detention Center, his grandmother continued to insist that she had no recollection of him hitting or otherwise striking her.

"He would never hit me on purpose," she maintained, "never." Instead, her grandson had accidentally knocked her over, and she had fallen to the ground, striking her head on the fireplace. "They've got him tarred and feathered," she said. "They have him ready for the gallows."

~~~~~

Back in Gainesville, the Mortar Board Honor Society established a memorial for the five slain students on September 20. Five live oak trees were planted on the UF campus near the entrance to Smathers Library, one for each victim, along with a metal plaque listing their names and containing the inscription "In Memory of the Fellow Students Whose Lives Were Needlessly Lost in August 1990".

~~~~~

A few weeks later, Brevard County State Attorney Norm Wolfinger pushed forward with Humphrey's prosecution. On October 10, following a one-hour deliberation, the six-person jury reached its verdict finding Humphrey guilty of the reduced charge of battery on an elderly person. Although he denied that the Gainesville murder investigation had any influence on his office's treatment of the Humphrey case, Wolfinger acknowledged that the swift trial and conviction would aid the investigation.

"If, in fact, a prime suspect is Edward Humphrey, they would have additional time to continue their investigation without making an arrest," Wolfinger said after the verdict.

Despite the verdict, Humphrey's mother, Elna Humphrey, proclaimed her son's innocence.

"They are still playing this game with trumped-up charges," she said. "They are trumped up in Gainesville and they are trumped up here. It's been such a victimization and traumatization for us."

Humphrey's grandmother expressed similar outrage.

"They didn't believe me. I'm the only one who knows," she said, her voice alternating between sorrow and spitefulness. "I have a crippled grandson who is being railroaded in Hell until they find the Gainesville murderer," she exclaimed, her face twisted in a mix of anger and sadness.

The day after Humphrey's conviction, an *Associated Press* article ran in the *Los Angeles Times* and other newspapers around the country under the title *Florida Slaying Suspect Found Guilty in Beating*, further etching Humphrey's name into the minds of the public.

A more local paper, the October 11 edition of the *Miami Herald*, added another twist to the case by featuring a story with the headline, *Louisiana Case is Similar to Killings in Gainesville.* The article asserted that the Gainesville task force had "renewed its interest" in the Shreveport triple-homicide of the Grissom family. It cited numerous similarities between the Gainesville and Shreveport crime scenes, including that all of the female victims were young, petite brunettes; the killer used tape during the crimes, but then removed it afterward; and the killer used cleaning liquids at the sites to scrub the rape victims' bodies and destroy evidence. Sgt. Dick Gerard, spokesman for the task force, downplayed the similarities.

“They have reviewed that case as well as a number of others,” he said. “It’s not any more significant.”

Around the same time that the Shreveport case surfaced in the media, the task force’s efforts to build a case against Humphrey for the Gainesville murders suffered a significant blow. DNA testing on blood and hair samples taken from Humphrey failed to match his DNA profile to samples recovered from the Gainesville crime scenes.

A few days later, on November 15, Humphrey appeared in a Titusville courtroom again, this time for sentencing. He nodded as his grandmother blew him a kiss, and then he took his place at the defense table to learn his fate. Under the state sentencing guidelines, Judge Theron Yawn could sentence Humphrey to a range of punishment spanning from probation on the lenient side, up to 22 months in prison on the harshest extreme. Although it was Humphrey’s first offense, the judge did not hesitate in sentencing him to the maximum term of 22 months confinement in the Correctional Mental Health Institution, a mental hospital in Chattahoochee, with 14 months of probation to follow. It was like pouring salt on the wounds of his outraged family.

“It’s a charade of justice,” his grandmother complained afterward, deeply regretting that the police had ever been called the night of the argument with her grandson.

~~~~~

As Thanksgiving came and went, a frustrated Gainesville community tried to remain patient with the Gainesville Ripper investigation, while the victims’ families struggled to balance their feelings of grief and frustration.

“We feel kind of dead,” said Christina Powell’s mother, Patricia. “I don’t know how else to put it.”
~~~~~

"We know absolutely nothing. Nothing at all," Sonja's father, Jim Larson, stated. "There's some agitation with that. The only thing we know is that our child was killed."

Although keenly aware of the community's frustration, investigators and prosecutors resisted putting a timetable on solving the case.

"This isn't television," pointed out Win Phillips of the Sheriff's Office. "It's been time-consuming, labor-intensive, and costly."

Michael West, the Mississippi forensic expert who examined the crime scenes, supported the methodical process despite how incredibly slow-moving it seemed to the public.

"This person didn't leave them anything to work with," West explained. "He didn't wake up one morning and decide to kill. He did some planning and was careful."

Captain Steve Bodiford, a homicide investigator at the Leon County Sheriff's Office, also sympathized with the task force's plight. He knew what challenges they faced. Bodiford had worked the Ted Bundy serial killings a decade earlier.

"They're in a hell of bind," Bodiford asserted. "What do you do? If you have no evidence, you run all the leads down and try to develop new ideas. It's tough."

His team of detectives had been fortunate to apprehend Bundy within four weeks of the killer's Tallahassee crimes, catching a lucky break through Bundy's desperation and carelessness. He understood the importance of finding solid leads and the diminishing chances of doing so with the passage of time.

"What goes away is your potential witnesses' recollection of the events," Bodiford explained. He summed up what the Gainesville task force most needed with one word.

"Luck," he said.

~~~~~

As the investigation continued into its fourth month, task force members grew increasingly frustrated. The diminishing morale and disappointment was palpable despite the traditional cheer of the approaching Christmas holiday. Chief Wayland Clifton projected optimism to the public, while stressing the need to remain vigilant.

"Our assumption is the killer could strike again," he cautioned.

Around the same time, psychologist John Philpin prepared a psychological profile of the killer, concluding that his criminal acts had escalated over time.

> *He probably has done break-ins before – maybe just creepy-crawly trips where he entered, moved things around and perhaps removed innocuous objects.*
>
> *The whole idea of watching a woman, coming in from the outside, invading her privacy, would appear to be a significant part of the ritual and the related fantasy system. This guy may have a juvenile record for this type of offense.*

It would not take long for the accuracy of his conclusion to be tested.
~~~~~

Chapter 14

1990

Marion County & Alachua County

After officials learn of his past escapes, the robbery suspect is treated as an "extreme escape risk" in the Marion County Jail. A memorandum establishing security protocol for him warns: "Do not be taken in by him. He has nothing to lose." The resulting strict security rules require that he be moved to a different cell every day, and guards check on him every 15 minutes. In spite of the tight security, or perhaps to spite his jailers, one night the prisoner attempts to escape by throwing his cell's toilet through the window. However, the plexiglass window does not break.

At his September 17, 1990, appearance in Marion County court, the prisoner pleads guilty to the Ocala Winn-Dixie robbery charge, surprising both the prosecutors and judge. Judge John Futch questions him carefully to make sure that he understands the proceeding and the meaning of his guilty plea, but the prisoner remains steadfast in his decision.

"I disturbed the peace of this county," he tells the judge, "and I am guilty, sir. Y'all judge me as you see fit. If you see anything in me -- and I wonder it myself -- that's worth saving, then maybe there's hope for me, but I don't know. Maybe I'm not worthy."

In a letter to the Marion County court, hoping to elicit leniency for her son, the prisoner's mother describes the hurdles and abuse he faced in the family home.

He was an abused child. From the day he was born, my husband was jealous of him. He never wanted me to hold him or show him love in his presence. I would have to write a book to tell you all that we as a family have suffered because of my husband's jealousy.

He was told from the time he could understand that he would be dead or in jail before he reached 15 years of age. His self-esteem was destroyed by his dad's constant belittling.

In another letter, his grandmother describes him as unpredictable.

He was a good boy. He changes just like the clouds in the sky. Some days it was sunny. And some days it was stormy and rainy.

The pleas of leniency do little to sway the court. After factoring in the prisoner's lengthy criminal record, including multiple robberies and the attempted murder of his father, Judge Futch sentences him to life imprisonment as a habitual felony offender.

While serving his sentence, the prisoner religiously follows news coverage of the Gainesville killings. He watches one TV news report with his cellmate. When the reporter states that the killer "may still be out there," the prisoner remarks with a wry smile, "If he is still out there, we are safe in here." He also mentions that he had stayed at a campground while in Gainesville and confidently announces that the police will "never catch the Gainesville killer."

Chapter 15

January -- February 1991

Gainesville/Indialantic/Shreveport

"*They were terrified of their dad . . . and they used to beg me to leave him*" (Claudia Rolling)

"*We lived in terror in that house*" (Danny Rolling)

Along with the New Year, a promising new suspect appeared on the task force's radar: a drifter already in custody in another jurisdiction for armed robbery. Shreveport detectives contacted their counterparts on the Gainesville task force and informed them that they suspect the drifter as the perpetrator of the 1989 Grissom family triple-homicide. Shreveport resident Cindy Dobbin, who met the drifter 15 years earlier at the United Pentecostal Church, called in a tip to the Shreveport Police Department that first put him on their radar as a suspect in the Grissom murders.

In following up the tip, Shreveport detectives noticed that striking parallels could be drawn between the Gainesville student killings and the murder of the Grissom family. Julie Grissom shared many of the same characteristics as the female victims in Gainesville: young, white female, around five feet four inches tall, shoulder length brown hair, and a college student. Like the female victims in Gainesville, after her death, Julie was positioned by her killer, who left her posed in a sexually suggestive manner on her bed. Julie and Sean Grissom had the same type of stab wounds near the center of their backs as the female victims in Gainesville, and like Christi Powell, Christa Hoyt, and Tracy Paules in Gainesville, Julie had been raped by her assailant. All three Shreveport victims were killed by a large-blade knife like the one used in the Gainesville murders. As in Gainesville, the killer in Shreveport tried to destroy evidence, putting Julie's underwear and other articles of her clothing in her washing machine and starting the wash cycle, as well as cleaning up Julie's body with paper towels. And like the Dawn liquid soap used to douche some of the Gainesville victims, Julie's killer had used vinegar to try to eradicate evidence left on her body. Additionally, like the Gainesville victims, Julie and Sean Grissom's wrists were bound with duct tape, which the killer removed after their deaths. However, while he took most of the tape with him when he left the Grissom crime scene, he left behind one piece on Julie's bedroom night stand, apparently overlooking it in his haste to leave the scene.

Despite the encouraging new lead, task force commanders directed their investigators to keep working every lead in the case, cautioning them to not get caught up in the "roller coaster ride" of the investigation. They pointed out how everyone had "got all worked up" when Steven Bates surfaced as a suspect, only to be disappointed when that lead did not pan out.

Although the three Gainesville crime scenes were remarkably clean with respect to recoverable evidence, Captain Ward stressed that despite the killer's careful planning and attempts to sanitize the murder sites, he had made two mistakes. The first was that he left tool-marks on some of the doors. The second and more important was that he failed to destroy all traces of semen at the crime scenes, including in a pair of panties and paper towels at the first scene, in Christa Hoyt's vagina at the second, and in Tracy Paules's rectum at the third. The mistakes left an opening for the task force and they hoped to exploit that chink in the killer's seemingly impenetrable armor. Captain Ward emphasized the need to obtain blood and hair samples from the newest suspect so that the FDLE could conduct proper testing to confirm or eliminate him as being present at the crime scenes.

Around the same time, the task force received some unwelcome news. Test results of semen samples recovered from the crime scenes failed to link Edward Humphrey to the Gainesville murders. The analysis identified the crime scene semen as related to blood type B, inherently distinguishable from Humphrey's blood type A. Despite the results, investigators declined to eliminate Humphrey as a suspect in the killings.

~~~~~

The night of January 22, 1991, Marion County jail officials contacted the task force with some good news. Earlier that evening, the prison dentist pulled a tooth for the suspect that had been bothering him. After removing the tooth, the jail medical staff packed the resulting hole in his mouth with gauze, and jail guard Donna Borgioni retrieved the tooth and bloody gauze from the jail infirmary afterward. They were already on their way to an FDLE laboratory for DNA testing. However, State Attorney Len Register warned the investigators not to pin too much hope on a possible DNA match. Even if a match could be made, DNA evidence was relatively new and unfamiliar to jurors. When the case went to trial, the jury might not understand the science or significance of DNA analysis. Recognizing that possibility, Register encouraged the team to continue its attempts at procuring other evidence that would tie the suspect to Gainesville.

Meanwhile, Gainesville Police Chief Wayland Clifton publicly addressed rumors that the task force had zeroed in on another promising suspect.

"I think we see the light at the end of the tunnel," he said. "We are looking very specifically at a certain individual. We're making substantial progress."

Two days later, anonymous sources identified 36-year-old Danny Harold Rolling as the task force's primary target, and the January 25 edition of the *Gainesville Sun* featured the headline, *Slaying Suspect in Ocala Jail Since September*. The article noted that the "polite" and "clean-cut" Rolling had been held in the Marion County Jail since September 7, 1990, after being arrested for the armed robbery of a Winn-Dixie supermarket in Ocala.
~~~~~

Rolling's Inmate Photo 1991

~~~~~~

As the news of Rolling's identification as a suspect in the Gainesville murders spread, his former neighbors in Shreveport, Louisiana expressed mixed reactions, but all remembered him as a peculiar loner.

"You might see him jog down the street dressed like Rambo," Gary Flowers recalled. "He did all kinds of things you just don't expect to see an adult do. He was so much on a child's level. There is no doubt he was strange."

Flowers recounted how, dressed in a bandanna, boots, and camouflage pants, the 6'2", 180 pounds "Rambo"
~~~~~~

would lift weights in the yard and sing songs to neighborhood children while playing his guitar.

"He was almost so nice with the neighborhood kids that it was eerie. It seemed strange for a man his age."

His wife recalled how Rolling let neighborhood kids play on his weight bench, all the while carefully watching to make sure none of them were hurt by a falling barbell.

"The kids loved him," she said.

Not surprisingly, Rolling's parents expressed shock at the news of their son's suspicion of murder.

"We're heartbroken over this," his father, James Rolling, stated flatly. "He may be disturbed, but he ain't guilty of that," his father insisted.

Rolling's mother seemed even more stunned.

"We are just sick over this," Claudia Rolling said. She compared the media frenzy focusing on her son to its previous treatment of Edward Humphrey. "They've destroyed him and his family like they're destroying my family. I'm so upset I can't talk about it anymore."

Humphrey's family knew exactly what she was going through.

"I hope they don't do to that family what they've done to this one," Elna Hlavaty said. "They haven't convicted him and yet they're putting him through what they put my grandson through. War prisoners are treated better than my grandson."

The public demonization of Rolling gave Humphrey's brother, George, a feeling of déjà vu, like his family's name was being dragged through the mud once again.

"I've been on one hell of a ride, and I don't know which way is up now," he said. "What we've gone through has changed all of us irrevocably. The Rolling family is now the focus of the nation's anger and fear."

George Humphrey's anger centered on the police and prosecutors' failure to maintain the integrity of the investigation, allowing leaks of confidential case information without tying their suspicions to anything substantive.

"Why can't they come up with some conclusive evidence before it all gets out? It's infuriating to me. If these investigators screw up again, someone needs to be held accountable."

His resentment and indignant reaction provided a glimpse of the emotional toll the experience had exacted from him and other family members.

> I'm shaken to the core. People who are your true friends won't say anything good because they don't want to be linked to a possible mass murderer. People who aren't that close just jump into the limelight. The picture that is painted is completely distorted.
>
> There's a lot of hidden motives. The police will leave doubt about whether my brother is a suspect until the very end to cover themselves.
>
> . . . . .
>
> They used my brother because he was mentally ill. The news media is like a dog: you wave a bone in front of them and they will jump. It was the law enforcement people who ruthlessly went after my brother.

Both members of the Humphrey family remained bitter about how the media, law enforcement, and the courts handled the investigation, particularly how they had vilified Ed without a bit of empathy.

"They're treating him as if he were convicted – tarred, feathered, and ready for the gallows," continued Elna Hlavaty. "But he didn't do anything. He's just another handicapped boy, and the law enforcement people are like hunters tracking down an injured animal."

"My brother wasn't well off mentally to begin with," George Humphrey pointed out angrily. "And this has rattled him to his foundations. He's so sensitive to what other people think about him, and here he was portrayed to the world as a mass murderer. He became the outlet for everyone's fear, and the police couldn't just come out and say, 'We messed up.' I don't think Ed will ever get over this."

~~~~~

As detectives delved deeper into Danny Rolling's past, they began uncovering fragments of a damaged personality. Born in the middle of the night on May 26, 1954, in Shreveport, Louisiana, Rolling's arrival was not an altogether happy occasion. His father, James Harold Rolling, had not wanted a child, and did not welcome the news when his 19-year-old bride became pregnant two weeks after their marriage. Claudia Rolling had been abused by her husband during the pregnancy, including being choked and shoved down a flight of stairs, and the stressful environment culminated in a difficult delivery that required the use of forceps to pull Danny from the birth canal. During the extraction, pressure from the forceps ruptured some veins in the infant's head leaving marks there that lasted nearly a year.

A few months after Danny's birth, Claudia became pregnant again, and Kevin Rolling was born on August 15, 1955. Throughout both pregnancies, arguments and abuse from James created a hostile, often hazardous, home
~~~~~

environment. When the physical and emotional torment became too much, Claudia took the children and left her husband multiple times, sometimes for days or weeks, but she always ended up coming back to him. She filed for separation when the boys were toddlers, but she could not bring herself to go through with a divorce. Instead, she moved back in with James and the abuse continued. When Danny was five, Claudia contemplated suicide by shooting herself, but she pointed the gun away at the last second and the bullet missed, burrowing into the hard surface of the floor instead of the soft tissue of her brain.

Not long after that, Danny fell off the back doorstep and hit his head on the concrete steps below. His eyes rolled back in his head and the impact made a “big dent” in his forehead. He did well his first couple of years in school, but then failed the third grade, a failure he attributed to frequent absences due to consecutive bouts with the mumps, measles, croup, and tonsillitis that cumulatively left him as thin as a skeleton. After being held back, his grades plummeted to D’s and F’s. School counselors attributed his poor performance to an inferiority complex with aggressive tendencies and lack of impulse control.

When he was 9, a cousin visiting from out of town sexually molested the young Rolling. Although he never wanted to talk about it, Rolling insisted that it happened only once. The lack of family support was soon equaled by a lack of spiritual guidance. The Rolling family regularly attended Sunset Acres Church of God, just down the road from their house, until his father abruptly decided to stop going when Danny was about 10. The next year Rolling walked in on his parents having a heated argument. Claudia locked herself in a bathroom and nearly slit her wrists with a razor before James managed to yank it out of her hand.

Throughout Danny’s childhood, James ruled the house with an iron fist. Danny and Kevin were not allowed to have friends over and they were not permitted to sit on the home’s only couch. Only their father could sit there. James often started arguments with Claudia and constantly belittled the boys both in public and at home. The family could never relax when James was around because of his frequent, volatile mood swings. Everyone walked on eggshells trying to avoid triggering his unpredictable temper.

The day before Danny started school as a seventh grader at Oak Terrace Junior High, his father decided he needed a haircut. Ignoring his son's pleading, James shaved his head nearly bare, and Danny was viciously mocked and teased by the other kids at school, who taunted him by calling him "Sasquatch" and "Bigfoot". It was a humiliation that he would never forget.

At Woodlawn High School in Shreveport, Danny enjoyed history and played in the school band, but he dropped out during his junior year. When he was 14, a friend introduced him to something that changed him forever, and not for the better. One summer night, James Anderson snuck over to Danny's house and told him he wanted to show him something. Curious, Danny followed as Anderson jumped over the fence into a neighbor's backyard.

"Take a look at this," Anderson told him, motioning to the neighbor's bathroom window.

Danny peered into the window and froze. The girl next door, a pretty cheerleader at school, was stepping out of the shower and drying herself with a lavender towel. Mesmerized, Rolling instantly became addicted to the experience. Peeping in windows became something he felt compelled to do over and over again, and he would continue doing it for the rest of his life.

~~~~~

During a period of depression when he was 15, Danny slit his own wrists. He had learned how to do so after watching his mother do the same thing several years earlier. *I tried*, he wrote on the bathroom mirror with her lipstick, *I just can't make it*.
~~~~~

~~~~~

He dropped out of high school after his sophomore year and enlisted in the Air Force in June 1971 as a 17-year-old. After completing basic training at Lackland Air Force Base in Texas, he served as a Security Police Officer for the Strategic Air Command at Homestead Air Force Base in Florida. He served on active duty for a total of 19 months, ultimately achieving the rank of Airman First Class, but he also repeatedly received disciplinary punishments for offenses ranging from failure to obey orders, to use of marijuana, to theft. He began drinking a lot in addition to doing drugs. The next year, he received a general discharge for the recurring behavioral problems and an "underlying immature personality."

Following his discharge, Danny returned to the family home, a small, white house on a corner lot at 6314 West Canal Boulevard in Shreveport. He sought out spiritual guidance by becoming active in the United Pentecostal Church of Shreveport, where he was baptized and attended services five days a week. He joined the church choir, drove the church bus for the handicapped, and dressed as the Easter Bunny for the church holiday celebration. A fellow member of the church congregation later described Danny as a "nice guy who was very people oriented."

It was during this period of his life that he developed a romantic relationship with a young woman from church, Omatha Ann Halko, whose mother had died in a train wreck when she was five. Danny believed that the "very sweet" Omatha had been sent to him by God in answer to his prayers to relieve his loneliness. He was smitten with her at first sight, and they married four months later on September 7, 1974. Within a year, Omatha gave birth to a daughter, Kiley Danielle Rolling, and they appeared to be a happy family. But Danny changed after the birth of their daughter, returning to drugs and peeping in windows, behavior he blamed on his wife's "frigid" attitude towards sex.
~~~~~

In 1976, Danny abruptly left Omatha and Kiley for nearly a month. When he returned, he offered no explanation for his absence other than telling Omatha that he had been in Florida. Less than a year later, Omatha had had enough. She left him in 1977, taking Kiley with her. Although their relationship had always been rocky, Danny was devastated by the separation and plagued by feelings of inadequacy and abandonment. That same year, the tips of the middle and ring fingers on Danny's left hand were amputated as a result of an accident while operating a bread slicing machine. It became a cruel, constant reminder of the failure of his marriage.

Chapter 16

Winter 1991 -- Summer 1991

Alachua/Marion/Hillsborough County

"It is unsettling to see someone who looks like a puppy dog, when he's really a dragon."

(Melanie Schiro, UF journalism student at the time of the student murders)

On January 25, 1991, five months after the five student murders, the Gainesville task force publicly named Danny Harold Rolling as the "prime suspect" in the Gainesville Ripper case. However, investigators in Shreveport declined to do the same for the Grissom family murders.

"To protect the integrity of the Shreveport case, this department will not discuss investigative leads, possible suspects or types of evidence," said Capt. Marshal Nelson of the Shreveport Police Department.

Although he often jogged at the same track as Julie Grissom, and the "quick tempered" Rolling had exploded when fired from his job at Pancho's restaurant only a mile from the Grissom home on the day of the murders, detectives lacked sufficient evidence to charge him.

~~~~~

On February 4, in an effort to stop information leaks that had plagued the investigation almost from the start and which had, most recently, prematurely disclosed Danny Rolling's name, task force leaders from all of the participating law enforcement agencies sent a letter to Florida newspapers and television news stations requesting cooperation from the media.
~~~~~

> *Our primary concern focuses on the apparent release of information by unknown individuals who are identified in media accounts only as "sources close to the investigation" or similar references. Such unauthorized releases have in some instances been inaccurate or incomplete, and therefore misleading to the public. In addition, we must emphasize, whether inaccurate or not, these premature unauthorized reports could severely hamper the investigation and cause irreparable damage to the prosecution of any suspect or suspects ultimately charged with these crimes.*

Despite the efforts at damage control, the harm had already been done to Edward Humphrey and his family. Larry Tuner, president of the Florida Association of Criminal Defense lawyers, noted the lynch mob mentality that had made Humphrey into a monster.

"In the minds of many, he was certainly convicted," Turner said. "The attitude at the time was, 'Let's convict the S.O.B. and get it over with."

With Danny Rolling now identified as the prime suspect, the hasty judgments of the reporters and investigators who had condemned Edward Humphrey in the court of public opinion began to face their own public scorn.

Several weeks later, FDLE agents appeared at Rolling's jail cell with a search warrant authorizing them to obtain DNA and other bodily evidence samples from him. Over the next 90 minutes, the agents took head hair, pubic hair, and blood samples to compare to DNA obtained at the Gainesville crime scenes. They also took footprints, handprints, and fingerprints.

Now nearly 60 officers strong, the task force continued following up close to 6,000 leads, but concentrated most of its efforts on gathering evidence against Rolling and Humphrey, including one tip that might provide the much-sought-after link between the two men. Gainesville resident Mary Underwood told police that the day before the first two victims were found, she stopped at a red light while driving her husband to Shands Hospital for heart treatment. When she looked over at the car in the lane next to her, she saw Humphrey sitting in the front passenger seat. When she looked over, he leaned in front of the driver and offered her 25 cents for two cigarettes. The light turned green and both cars continued on their way, but she later realized that the driver was Danny Rolling.

While task force detectives were shifting much of their focus to Rolling, Edward Humphrey continued serving his sentence in the State Mental Hospital in Chattahoochee, Florida. In letters to his family in late February and early March, he discussed how deeply the investigation, prosecution, and incarceration had affected him.

> *This experience has been the hardest of my life. I miss being free.*
>
> *I miss those great pancakes you make, Grandma, with Buttersworth syrup and the scrambled eggs and bacon.*
>
> . . . . .
>
> *All the people who think I'm just crazy are wrong. I'm not crazy. I just have to take a medication to keep my mind and*

> *body working together. If Grandma is still talking to the press tell her to tell them how before this illness I played football for a year and a starter and took seven classes a day and had a 3.5 GPA.*
>
> . . . . .

Most of his letters ended with a similar message:

> *Please do your best to get me out of this mess. It's really not fair what has happened to me.*

On March 12, the FDLE forensic laboratory finished its fingerprint and DNA analysis, concluding that none of the sample prints taken from Rolling in jail matched the latent prints obtained from the crime scenes. More importantly, however, a DNA profile obtained from semen recovered from vaginal swabs of Christa Hoyt matched Rolling's DNA so closely that there was only a 1 in 3,000,000 chance that it belonged to someone else. Additionally, fibers from the ski mask recovered at Rolling's campsite matched fibers found on a piece of duct tape recovered from the Gatorwood Apartments crime scene, and tool marks left on the door at Sonja Larson and Christi Powell's Williamsburg apartment matched the blade width and tip characteristics of a screwdriver found at Rolling's campsite. Further analysis would eventually connect the screwdriver to all three murder sites.

Investigators also gathered evidence suggesting that Rolling came into contact with at least some of the five slain students shortly before their murders. A Walmart receipt recovered from Sonja and Christi's apartment showed a purchase made from the Gainesville store on Archer Road near SW 34th Street on August 20, 1990. The transaction took place at register 11 at 6:03 p.m. At precisely the same time at nearby register 22, someone purchased the same brand and type of tent found at Rolling's campsite. Detectives also obtained security camera recordings at Vern's Kwik Shop, a convenience store located on SW 34th Street less than a block from Sonja Larson's apartment and directly across the street from Rolling's camp. The video footage showed Sonja entering the store at 9:28 p.m. on August 25, and recorded Rolling in the store several times the day before. Additional surveillance footage showed Rolling in the store at 12:05 a.m., 6:00 p.m., 6:30 p.m., 9:30 p.m., and 9:38 p.m. on August 24. Christa Hoyt had last been seen alive at 9:28 p.m. that same night when she stopped at the same convenience store on her way home after playing racquetball with her friend, Paul Schwartz.

~~~~~

FDLE special agents Cindy Barnard and Steve Davenport arrived at the Marion County Jail on April 17 bearing two arrest warrants for Rolling for the burglaries he committed in Tampa in early September 1990. After agent Barnard explained the probable cause evidence supporting the warrants, Rolling remarked that he had been "stupid" to use the telephone at one of the burglarized residences, but commented that it had been a "bad day" and he "needed to talk to someone." Wary of conducting an unlawful interrogation, the agents advised Rolling that they did not want to question him about any crimes without his attorney being present. Nonetheless, Agent Barnard mentioned that they knew Rolling had murdered the five Gainesville students.

"And how do you know that?" Rolling asked with raised eyebrows.

"We have DNA evidence, hair evidence, and other evidence," Barnard asserted confidently.

The agents let that fact sink in for a few moments. Then Agent Davenport spoke.
~~~~~

“Those murdered kids had parents who must have had a difficult time dealing with the deaths of their children,” Davenport said as if he was simply sharing his thoughts with his partner.

“Kind of like I had a hard time living up to my father’s expectations,” Rolling replied while staring down at the table.

“We know you were married and have a daughter,” Barnard said.

Rolling looked up. “You know a lot about me.”

“We know that you travelled to Kansas, Sarasota, and Tampa, and that you used the alias, ‘Michael Kennedy’”.

Rolling fixed his eyes on the agents, weighing the truth of their words in his mind.

“We know that you were in Gainesville and robbed a bank there. And we seized some interesting things from your campsite.”

Rolling shifted in his chair and sighed.

“My life is ruined,” he said quietly. “Do you think I’ll spend the rest of my life in prison?”

“I’d say that’s pretty likely,” Barnard answered.

“You know I will,” Rolling agreed, his voice growing louder. He sighed again, beginning a long release of pent-up emotion. “Everything would have turned out different if I’d moved into an apartment with my brother,” he lamented. “I never should have gone back to Shreveport after I got out of Parchman.”

He had the look of a man reliving unpleasant events from his life in the memory banks of his mind.

“I never got on track after my divorce,” he explained in a rueful tone. “I love my daughter and think about her every day. I hope she doesn’t know anything about me and what I’ve become.”

The three sat in silence for some time until Barnard asked if they could fingerprint him. When they finished taking prints, the agents handed Rolling their business cards.

"Let us know if there's ever anything we can do for you," they told him as prison guards came to take him away.

Rolling stood to leave, then paused.

"What's the bottom line?" he asked somberly.

Barnard and Davenport glanced at each other.

"We can't talk to you about the case without your attorney being present," Barnard replied. "We'd hate to have to put an innocent man in jail though."

Rolling looked confused.

"What are you talking about?" he asked.

"Ed Humphrey," Barnard advised.

Rolling sat back down in his chair. He fidgeted as he wrestled with what he should say, or whether he should say anything else at all.

"My lawyer's gonna kill me for this," he finally muttered. "I'm going to tell you two things," he announced holding up one finger. "Number one, I've never met Humphrey and I've never seen him except in newspaper photos. Number two, you need to clear that man's name."

With that, Rolling stood up again and shook Davenport's hand.

"God bless you," Rolling said, then guards escorted him out the door.

~~~~~

On May 21, the Shreveport Police Department announced that its detectives were investigating Rolling in connection with the Grissom family murders.
~~~~~

“Because of his connection to both the Shreveport and Gainesville areas, we have, of course, looked at him as a possible suspect,” stated Lt. Gary Pittman, chief of the department’s homicide unit. However, Pittman stopped short of naming Rolling as the prime suspect in the killings, instead referring to him as a “possible suspect” and maintaining that the Shreveport police could not yet name him or anyone else as the prime or only suspect.

Meanwhile, Rolling’s mother continued to defend her son, who she had recently visited in the Ocala jail.

“I saw no guilt in my son,” she said. “If they had concrete evidence, he would have been charged long ago. It’s a witch hunt,” she insisted. “He’s been accused, tried, convicted, and all but executed – without even being charged. They concentrated on Danny, and they’re letting the guilty person run free out there. And I pray that he does not kill again.”

Danny’s father was strangely silent.

Despite naming Rolling as the prime suspect in their case, Alachua County prosecutors announced that they would seek grand jury indictments against both Rolling and Edward Humphrey. Addressing why indictments would be sought against both men, FDLE spokesman, John Joyce explained, “We feel like we have evidence that needs to be presented to a grand jury that we hope will lead to indictments against both of these people.”

The announcement raised the spirits of the victims’ families as well as many in the Gainesville community needing to vent their simmering indignation, wanting someone to direct their anger against. The investigation had not only exacted a profound psychological toll on the families and the greater Gainesville community, it had also come at a heavy financial cost. The year-old case, in which over 200 investigators combed through more than 6,500 leads, had now cost the taxpayers of Florida over 4.7 million dollars.

~~~~~

As the task force and prosecutors began preparing their case for the grand jury, Rolling continued to face criminal proceedings in both Marion County and Hillsborough County relating to the string of robberies he committed after leaving Gainesville. At a May 30 competency hearing in Marion County before Judge Thomas Sawaya, forensic psychiatrist William Corowin testified about his interview and examination of Rolling. Dr. Corowin recounted how Rolling told him about his history of substance and alcohol abuse, the former including the use of marijuana, cocaine, and crack cocaine during his time in Tampa, and the latter starting when he was seventeen while serving as security police in the Air Force.

Corowin also discussed how Rolling described seeing a "demon" one night while in bed with his wife. The bedroom window was partially open and a cold wind blew the curtains over him. He saw something outside "pouring into the house like black smoke" and then "different faces and forms" appeared in the darkness. Frightened, Rolling blurted out "Jesus" three times, causing the "demon" to retreat back through the window. Based on his interactions with Rolling, Dr. Corowin diagnosed him with antisocial personality disorder and a schizophrenic type of psychosis.

~~~~~

On June 13, 1991, corrections officers moved a closely guarded and heavily chained Edward Humphrey from the Corrections Mental Health Institution in Chattahoochee to the North Florida Reception Center in Lake Butler near Gainesville. The 19-year-old Humphrey looked forward to his scheduled release date of September 28.

~~~~~

On July 23, Judge Harry Lee Coe, affectionately known among the Hillsborough County legal community as "Hanging Harry" for his unwavering pro-prosecution
~~~~~

temperament, held a hearing in the consolidated criminal cases against Rolling arising from his Tampa area burglaries. Judge Coe heard testimony from several medical experts on the issue of whether Rolling should be deemed competent to stand trial for his offenses. Clinical psychologist Fred Farzanegan testified that after examining Rolling at the Hillsborough County Jail, he considered Rolling competent to stand trial. Sidney Merin, a clinical and neuropsychologist, testified next and reached the same conclusion, while also opining that Rolling had a schizotypical type of personality and antisocial personality traits. Psychiatrist Arturo Gonzalez likewise testified that Rolling appreciated and understood the charges against him and could conduct himself appropriately in court. Michael Maher, a general and forensic psychiatrist retained by the Public Defender's Office, came last and testified on behalf of the defense. Dr. Maher testified that Rolling was not competent to stand trial because he suffered from a personality disorder and an unspecified affective disorder. Assistant State Attorney Cass Castillo asked Dr. Maher whether he thought Rolling could be faking mental illness in order to avoid facing the charges against him. Maher categorically rejected the suggestion.

> It has been my experience that it is unusual for a criminal defendant to fake mental illness in order to attempt to seek psychiatric hospitalization. Specifically, in this case, I would be shocked to discover evidence that the defendant is doing that. It is my conclusion that rather than attempting to look bad and fake looking sick, he is much more likely to attempt to try to put on the most normal, least psychiatrically disturbed façade that he can muster.

After considering all of the experts' testimony, Judge Coe ruled Rolling competent to stand trial, concluding that he had a "rational as well as factual understanding of the charges against him."

~~~~~

On August 21, ahead of the one-year anniversary of their children's murders, the parents of Sonja, Christi, Christa, Manny, and Tracy released a written statement to the public through the Gainesville Police Department.

We are angry, very angry, they wrote. *Know that the pain of our loss will never go away. Our lives have been irreparably altered for the worse. Our children were wonderful, loving, beautiful, intelligent, and delightful. Do not expect us to forgive the person(s) responsible; some of us will, some of us will not.*

A member of Christi Powell's family told reporters that her parents "really don't have revenge in their hearts," but wanted "this monster removed from society so he can't do this to another innocent victim."

The next day, detectives took blood, hair, and saliva samples from Rolling pursuant to a warrant obtained by Shreveport police investigating the Grissom murders. The investigators intended to compare the fluid samples to saliva recovered at the crime scene from a bite mark on Julie Grissom's breast. The affidavit filed in support of the warrant cited several evidentiary grounds for conducting the testing, including that Rolling lived in Shreveport at the time of the Grissom murders and jogged at the same Southern Hills park as Julie Grissom; that on the day of the murders Rolling had been fired from his job at Pancho's restaurant, located a mile from the Grissom home; that hair evidence recovered from a car which Rolling stole in Florida matched hair found at the Grissom crime scene; and that the saliva swabbed from Julie's breast came from a type B blood secretor.
~~~~~

While Rolling faced the consequences of his crimes in Marion and Hillsborough County, Edward Humphrey's attorneys sought to reduce or set aside his 22-month sentence by appeal. Contending that an excessive sentence had been imposed solely due to the influence of the Gainesville case, Assistant Public Defender Michael Becker wrote in Humphrey's appellant brief that *he has been forced to exist in jail in solitary confinement not for the crime which he stands convicted, but for other matters that are beyond his control, namely the fact that he has been branded as a suspect in the Gainesville murders*. However, on August 23, the Fifth District Court of Appeal rejected Humphrey's claim and upheld his sentence. Although not surprised by the ruling, public defender J.R. Russo remained adamant that the sentence imposed "was completely out of line with other cases we see through here every day." Clearly frustrated for his client, Russo explained that "anyone else would have gotten probation."

Chapter 17

Fall 1991 – Summer 1992

"The monster that they said he was . . ."
(Inmate Russell Binstead)

August 25, 1991, marked the one-year anniversary of the discovery of the first Gainesville murder victims. Reflecting back, FDLE agent Cindy Barnard recalled the horror of seeing the three crime scenes first-hand.

"It's such a horrible way to die – people felt safe in their homes and 15 minutes later they're fighting with someone to stay alive," she said. "They could have been your classmates, sorority sister, your own sister, or somebody you worked with. And if everyone were honest with themselves, they would say, 'That could have been me.'"

The next day, officer Ray Barber of the Gainesville Police Department received a call from a reporter with the *Gainesville Sun*. The caller stated that he had seen a news report from WTVJ, a television station in Miami, featuring a woman claiming to be the girlfriend of Danny Rolling. The woman, 24-year-old Margret Harrington, displayed a duffel bag that had an identification tag with the name "Humphrey" along with Edward Humphrey's correct address and phone number. She claimed that Rolling had left the bag at her apartment. If true, the bag could be the link between Rolling and Humphrey that everyone was "looking for." After viewing the TV report, the caller went to Harrington's home and saw FDLE agents carrying out the duffel bag, a backpack, and some other items. But when the caller personally spoke to Harrington, she told him that she had made the entire story up.

"I lied. I'm not Danny Rolling's girlfriend," she said. "I like Danny Rolling and I want to know him. I tried once to meet him and call him, but I'm not really his girlfriend. I liked Ted Bundy and tried to talk to him, too."

When the caller asked her about the duffel bag, Harrington said that she had seen George Humphrey throwing some things into a dumpster at Humphrey's apartment complex. After he left, she dug the duffel bag out of the dumpster. Later, when TV reporters arrived at her house, she agreed to talk with them as "Rolling's girlfriend," hoping that Rolling would want to meet her after he saw the report.

On August 27, a public relations firm representing Edward Humphrey released a seven-minute interview of him taped at the North Florida Reception Center in Lake Butler. To portray him in the best possible light, Humphrey's new publicist convinced the warden to allow him to wear a collared shirt instead of his normal prison uniform. His brother brought a clean shirt for him to change into before taping the interview.

The publicist, Margaret Mackenzie, frowned when she saw Humphrey's buzz-cut prison haircut. She worried that Humphrey's shaved head made him look aggressive, certainly not the way they wanted him to come across in the interview. To lessen the impact, she suggested that he run his hand over his head and mention that he looked forward to getting a real haircut when he finished serving his sentence.

That night the interview ran on dozens of news reports throughout the state. In his first public comments since being convicted for assaulting his grandmother, and with less than a month left on his sentence, Humphrey reasserted his innocence in the Gainesville murders and speculated that he became a suspect for those crimes because of his behavior during the days immediately after the killings.

"I think at the time last August when I was there, I really wasn't normal because I was not on my medication, my Lithium, because I'm a manic depressive," he stated. "And because of that, I kind of stuck out in a crowd, and people recognized me because of that."

He also talked about his reaction when he learned that he was the main suspect in the Gainesville murders.

"I was horrified. I thought it was terrible that they could actually think that I could have anything to do with something like that. I haven't done anything wrong."

Humphrey explained that the incident with his grandmother that led to his arrest had simply been a misunderstanding that was blown out of proportion. He said that he always had a great relationship with his grandmother and that she had visited him every week during his confinement. He also discussed what he planned to do after being released.

"The first thing is I'm going to get my hair cut by a regular barber," he said, rubbing his hand across his head under Mackenzie's watchful eye. "I'm going to have my scars taken care of and get plastic surgery and have the rod removed from my leg. I'm going to spend a lot of time with my family, and I'm going to get with them to make up for the time that we missed while I was in prison. And I hope eventually to go back to school."

The following morning, a front-page article in the *Orlando Sentinel* included a photograph of Humphrey touching his head with the caption: *In an interview Humphrey said he is doing better and looking forward to a haircut by a regular barber*. The rehumanizing of Edward Humphrey had begun.

"He's been stereotyped by a moment in his life, which is not an accurate depiction of who Ed Humphrey is," Mackenzie explained afterward. "This was a strategic approach to introduce Ed Humphrey as he is today."

Back in Gainesville, Police Chief Clifton expressed confidence that the task force's efforts would secure an indictment from the grand jury.

"Our evidence is as strong as it can possibly get. I am 1,000 percent certain that we have the right person or people in custody on unrelated charges, and the November 4 grand jury will be very successful for us," Clifton boldly asserted.

~~~~~

On August 29, after three hours of deliberation, the jury in Rolling's Tampa armed robbery trial returned its verdict finding him guilty on all seven counts. As he listened to the verdict, Rolling looked over at his mother seated in the front of the courtroom gallery.

"It's okay, Mom," he assured her.

"I know," Claudia Rolling replied quietly, "And I love you."

Judge Harry Lee Coe set Rolling's sentencing hearing for October 11.

~~~~~

Having served more than a year in prison, Edward Humphrey was released from the Lake Butler Correctional Institution on September 18. Other than stopping for a haircut and shave on the way, he drove straight to the Orlando office of his attorney, Donald Lykkebak. Wearing a blue blazer, khaki pants, and red tie, and sporting his new clean-cut hair style, Humphrey appeared in front of members of the media in a small, 12th-floor conference room with his mother, brother, and grandmother by his side.

"I am flattered that you all came today to see my great new haircut," he joked, reading from a prepared statement. "I am still sometimes overwhelmed by all this interest from the media. I'm happy to be talking with you, but I hope this is the last time I have to do this."

He paused and looked around at the faces of his family.

"I am very, very happy to be free from prison today. My family has been wonderful to me. This has been a terrible year, but today it's finally over," he declared. "I want to get this year behind me and go on with my life. I am looking forward to being with my friends and enjoying my life."

After announcing that he planned on completing the terms of his fourteen-month probation by living with his brother in an apartment in Orlando, Humphrey gave way to his attorney. Lykkebak in turn denounced his client's imprisonment as a "raw deal" and "injustice." He projected confidence about the grand jury proceeding scheduled for November 2.

"I firmly believe that if the evidence is fairly and accurately presented to the grand jury, my client will not be indicted," he proclaimed.

He explained Humphrey's strange behavior at the time of the murders as entirely attributable to his having "stopped taking his Lithium at the wrong time and at the wrong place," an error in judgment for which he had "paid a very dear price."

"He's just a boy with a big smile and a good heart," Lykkebak said.

Although investigators had claimed that pubic hairs found at two of the Gainesville crime scenes linked Humphrey to the murders, Lykkebak dismissed the claim as wholly unsupportable.

"That is not evidence that is going to be recognized by any court in Florida," he asserted. "It does not identify Edward as having been at the scene."

Similarly dismissing the possibility that Humphrey helped Rolling commit the crimes, Lykkebak maintained that Humphrey had been driving back and forth between Gainesville and Indialantic at the time of the murders.

"If you apply logic and reason to this," he insisted, "there is absolutely no way these two people would ever get together and no evidence that they ever have been together."

His comments rang true. Despite their collective best efforts, task force investigators had been unable to link Rolling and Humphrey. Employees of a Jiffy Store on SW Archer Road, not far from the murder sites, were the closest they came. The witnesses recalled seeing Humphrey and Rolling in the store, but not at the same time and certainly not together.

The investigation of Humphrey had been driven by desperation, Lykkebak explained. The task force members had ignored reason in their haste to build a case against him.

"We're not asking for any apology," he said. "We're asking them to do their job fairly and honestly."

~~~~~

The same day as Humphrey's release, in nearby Marion County, Rolling received a life sentence plus 30 years as a habitual offender for the September 1990 robbery of an Ocala Winn-Dixie. Rolling showed little reaction to the sentence from Judge Thomas Sawaya, but stated "God bless the people of Florida, and Lord help me," after the judge announced the life imprisonment term.

A month later on October 18 in Hillsborough County, Judge Harry Lee Coe sentenced Rolling to three consecutive life sentences – one for each cashier he robbed -- plus 170 years for the string of robberies and burglaries committed in Tampa. In imposing the sentence, Coe stressed that he intended for it to ensure that Rolling would "not be given the
~~~~~

opportunity to see the light of day again." In response, Rolling told the court, "I guess I've always been a problem. I want to crawl under the woodwork somewhere, but I can't seem to find a crack."

On November 5, grand jury proceedings regarding Rolling and Humphrey's involvement in the five student murders commenced in a jury room on the fourth floor of the Alachua County Courthouse in Gainesville. The lead prosecutor, State Attorney Len Register, picked J.O. Jackson, head of the task force, to present details about the criminal case, and Steve Platt, head of the FDLE's crime lab, to discuss DNA and other pertinent scientific evidence.

Just over a week later on November 13, Ed Humphrey's "eccentric and gruff" grandmother, Elna Hlavaty, died of a heart attack following an argument with her daughter. The two had argued about a telephone conversation between Hlavaty and a *Florida Today* news reporter, an argument precipitated by the family's prior decision to decline talking to any reporters until after the Gainesville grand jury reached a verdict on whether to indict Edward Humphrey.

After collapsing in her Indialantic home on November 13, Hlavaty was rushed to Holmes Regional Medical Center in Melbourne where she died at 1:15 p.m. She had suffered a mild heart attack several weeks before, an attack her doctors attributed to hardening of her arteries and stress caused by the criminal investigation of her grandson.

"Grandmother is another victim of these crimes," George Humphrey said after the announcement of his 80-year-old grandmother's death. "Our whole family has been on edge this week because of the grand jury. Their decision literally means life or death for us."

Two days later, after only 30 minutes of deliberations, the Gainesville grand jury indicted Danny Rolling on five counts of first degree murder, three counts of sexual battery, and three counts of armed burglary. In announcing the indictment, State Attorney Len Register acknowledged the public's patience during the process.

"I know some have questioned why it took so long, but I think it's obvious to most of you that this is no typical case with the volume of information we're dealing with," he stated during a news conference.

Register's team had sought indictments against two men, but it obtained only one. The grand jury found the evidence presented against Edward Humphrey insufficient to support issuing an indictment against him. Although pubic hairs similar to Humphrey's were recovered at two of the crime scenes, DNA testing exonerated him. The jury deemed the evidence against Humphrey so weak that it not only declined to indict him, but also issued a "no true bill" conveying the jurors' conclusion that he had nothing to do with the Gainesville murders.

Humphrey and his family learned of the news while at a Melbourne funeral home hosting services for Humphrey's grandmother.

"We expected it," George Humphrey said in a voice projecting both relief and resentment. "But I feel in all this that we've been treated horribly unfairly and for no good reason. And the truth is, we are sick of it."

Still fuming about the hellish experience, he decried how his brother had been made a scapegoat and lashed out at law enforcement and the media.

"Once he was portrayed as a mass murderer, he became the outlet for everyone's fear. After that, the police could never come out and say, 'We messed up,' and that they had the wrong person." He thanked publicist Margaret Mackenzie and attorney Donald Lykkebak for saving his brother from being railroaded to death row while the "wheels of justice failed him".

Later that month, having helped rehabilitate Humphrey in the court of public opinion, MacKenzie and

Lykkebak appeared on the tabloid TV show, *A Current Affair*, on a segment about Ed Humphrey titled "Makeover of a Monster".

~~~~~

In March 1992, Rolling arrived in Tallahassee for yet another trial, this one in federal court for the robbery of the First Union Bank in Gainesville. On May 21, following convictions for possession of a firearm by a convicted felon and for bank robbery, he received his sentence. Prior to sentencing, Assistant United States Attorney Greg Miller told the court, "He is unsuitable ever to be released from prison. He shows a complete lack of remorse for the crimes he has committed."

Given his opportunity to address the court, Rolling initially broke out into song: "Jesus, I want to be more like You / and I just want You to know I'm trying / All my life I've known misery / then You came into my life and set me free / I love You, yes I do." Then he spoke to the judge:

> Your Honor, I think there's a lot of sorrow and plenty of misery to go around in this old world we live in today. And Mr. D.A. and you gentlemen, I don't hate you guys, I don't hate nobody. But I think we're looking to the wrong person for our answers and solutions to the problems in this world. We're looking to our fellow man, and we haven't done a very good job, have we, Judge? But if we could just look to our Creator, then we could find answers, but I suppose it's not in our nature to do that. But I want to thank you people for the way you have treated me and
~~~~~

ask you to pray for me. That's all
I wanted to say.

Whether annoyed or amused by Rolling's strange singing and dubious statement, U.S. District Judge Maurice Paul listened quietly for several minutes until Rolling finished. Then he calmly sentenced Rolling to life in prison.

With the federal case now resolved, the legal path was clear for Rolling to be arrested for the murders of Christi Powell, Sonja Larson, Christa Hoyt, Manny Taboada, and Tracy Paules.

Chapter 18

Summer -- Fall 1992

"God has forgiven me for killing them people. Why can't everybody else?" (Danny Rolling)

In early June 1992, Florida State Prison inmate Robert "Bobby" Lewis, a former Death Row inmate now serving a life sentence, wrote a letter to Sondra London, a pen-pal and confidante of several other inmates. In his letter, Lewis revealed that he had formed a friendship with Danny Rolling while working on W-Wing of the prison and that he planned to take advantage of his new colleague.

> *I plan on making a deal with the people hear [sic] that I will get his hole [sic] story . . . on two conditions. That I get out of prison for testifying against him and two the way I'm gone [sic] do it. I'm going to have him sign an agreement to give you the exclusive to his life story.*
>
> . . . . .
>
> *There is nothing this man has not told me.*
>
> . . . . .
>
> *[A]t the same time the prison will have to open the doors to you. Because you gone [sic] help them solve the case threw [sic] his story to you! The books, movies, tapes, will be worth a great deal of money – I want 33 1/3 for him – 33 1/3 for me 33 1/3*

> *for you . . . All this is not negotiable – send me an answer right back . . . if not then I go elsewhere. But this is my freedom and a lot of money. I'm gone [sic] let you have first chance.*

London, who turned her aspirations to true crime after a career in technical writing, had co-authored a book of fiction in 1997 with serial killer Gerard Schafer, a former boyfriend from high school. Since then she had become friendly with Lewis while writing about his escape from Death Row. Lewis, convicted for the January 1977 murder of Joseph Richards, was the only person in history to escape from Florida's Death Row. On November 18, 1978, he had walked out the front entrance of Florida State Prison in broad daylight. In the middle of the day, wearing a correctional officer's uniform that he had hidden in a visiting room and donning a fake moustache, Lewis calmly made his way to the main gate of the prison. He told the gate guard that his wife had been in a car accident and that someone was waiting outside to drive him to the hospital to see her. The guard did not hesitate in waving him through. Eleven days later, FBI agents captured Lewis in Santee, South Carolina. However, in a stroke of luck, his death sentence was overturned in 1982 and he had been resentenced to life imprisonment, plus six additional years for his escape.

Now, as his letter to London continued, Lewis encouraged her to contact Rolling and gave her advice on how best to approach him: *He got a big ego, your [sic] gone need to stroke: how good his writing is, how big this can be. Talk books, movies, T.V., gross, net, all that shit*. Aware of London's past emotional attachments to inmates, Lewis also advised her about how to go about writing Rolling's story, cautioning not to let her personal feelings get in the way of the truth:

> [W]rite about a killer as [to] what he is and let it fall where it will . . . you want to love & cuddle them . . . the public don't want poor killer stories especially one like [Rolling]. They want the raw stuff the dirt – the rest a lot of psychologists and so on would be interested in. But as a commercial product I don't think it sells good.

While reaching out to London to pique her interest in Rolling, Lewis also talked her up to Rolling, hoping to get him interested in working with her. The talks worked. On June 23, Rolling wrote the first of a series of letters to London offering her the chance to have exclusive access to his story. Through the reams of correspondence that followed, they would develop a close personal and professional relationship, including a collaboration on a book. But for now, they were still getting to know each other.

~~~~~

Meanwhile, on June 25, London received a second letter from Bobby Lewis updating her on information that Rolling had shared with him. Lewis proposed splitting with London 50/50 the proceeds of Rolling's story from any book, media, or movie deals, and cutting Rolling out completely. The next day, London called Lewis's attorney, Robert Link. She informed him that Rolling wanted her to write his story and would be making statements about the Gainesville homicides through her. Link advised her not to respond to Rolling's letter, warning that if his attorney, public defender Rick Parker, found out about the arrangement, he would stop Rolling from having any further communication with her whatsoever. London decided it was a risk worth taking. She wrote a reply to Rolling shortly thereafter, continuing an exchange of letters that would carry on throughout the year.
~~~~~

As their relationship grew, Rolling assured London that he would give her the real story about his life and crimes. He rejected her suggestion that he had already bared his soul to another writer, author and criminal profiler John Philpin, while being held in federal prison in Tallahassee. Rolling acknowledged having exchanged letters with Philpin and having briefly spoken to him on the phone, but he insisted that Philpin *did not get but a grain of sand compared to the beach I gave you*, and that *[a]nything he has come up with using me as an exclusive will have to be almost total FABRICATION*.

Bobby Lewis met with prison officials shortly before 3:00 p.m. on July 2. He knew that investigators were hungry for information about Rolling, and he intended to use their desperation to his advantage. He began by explaining how he had befriended Rolling when the two shared the same floor on W-Wing of the prison. Rolling had been upset about harassment and bullying at the hands of the guards that had been ongoing since his arrival at the prison.

"Why are they doing that to me?" Rolling asked.

"You got to understand that in prison, that's just part of it, for killing women, killing kids, stuff like that," Lewis explained. "Your case is similar to Ted Bundy's. You're going to have a lot of problems. You might as well settle back and get used to it."

"Well, God has forgiven me for killing them people. Why can't everybody else?" Rolling asked in reply.

The two men talked frequently after that initial exchange. Rolling shared his plan to escape from the Gainesville Jail if he could find a way to get sent back there, and he spoke about his fear of being moved to Q-Wing, which housed the electric chair. Rolling came up with a ruse to stay on W-Wing by pretending to attempt suicide. He made a noose and tied it around his neck, then twisted it down and laid on his bed. He looked up at Lewis.

"This don't hurt," Rolling assured him, "but it looks good. Wait until my face starts turning a little red and just holler for them."

Lewis waited and then yelled for the guards. The plan worked perfectly. Rolling stayed on W-Wing as a suicide risk.

Rolling confided to Lewis that deep-down he knew he would end up on Death Row, and he wanted to sell his story so that he could help his daughter financially. He also enjoyed all of the media attention about his case.

"I get a big kick out it," Rolling laughed. "I got all this publicity here in Florida. I'm a star. I'm a superstar. I got world attention. If only they knew what I've really done. This ain't nothing here. This is shit. This ain't nothing."

About ten days after his first meeting with prison officials, Lewis met with FDLE Agent Lee Strope and elaborated on the information that he had previously shared. In discussing Rolling's desire to help his daughter, Lewis called it his "main goal," stating: "He wanted to make sure that she wasn't treated like his daddy treated him, that she had some chance in life. He was pretty serious about that."

Stope met with inmate Russell Binstead the same day. Like Lewis, Binstead was angling to help himself out. He explained how curiosity had led to his first encounter with Rolling.

> They'd brought him in from North Florida Reception Center. They put him in a cell on the second floor of W-Wing where I was working as a runner. I just walked down at that point to see what he looked like. You know I'd read so much about him and heard so much about him I wanted to see just what he

> looked like. You know if he looked like the monster that they said he was.

Rolling talked to Binstead about escaping, but said that if he could not escape, he wanted to pursue an insanity defense. Binstead said that Rolling told him he had been able to elude capture so long because he stayed in the woods during the day and only came out at night because he was a "night creature."

In July 1992, Rolling snidely responded to a letter from a reporter at the *Florida Alligator* who had written asking him to discuss his feelings about the death penalty.

I am a man who has 5 life sentences and 170 years to serve in the grand ole state of Florida, Rolling wrote in reply. *So either someday I will be old and gray in prison and my heart gives out . . . or I'll be young and strong and ELECTROCUTED. Kinda speaks for itself, doesn't it kiddo?*

~~~~~

Bobby Lewis met with Gainesville task force investigators in Florida State Prison on October 1, 1992. Rolling had been impressed by the fact that Lewis escaped from Death Row, and he continued to divulge incriminating information to his prison confidante. Rolling knew that Lewis would be talking to investigators. He was "real methodical about anything he did," and instructed Lewis to give them a statement: "The ones I left with their legs spread laying on their back, on the floor with their legs spread wide open. I left a message there. They'll know what I'm talking about." Rolling also said to tell them that he used a screwdriver and grey duct tape while committing the crimes.

A few weeks later, Lewis met again with the investigators to provide them the latest information Rolling had shared. He spoke often about his father, blaming him for what he had done. Rolling called him a "psychopathic sadist" and despairingly told Lewis, "I never wanted to be like
~~~~~

him, but I'm much, much worse." Rolling also worried that the audio tape he recorded in the woods would be especially incriminating, particularly the hunting instructions to his brother. According to Lewis, Rolling "wanted people to believe that it was a deer that he was talking about killing . . . by making it bleed to death," when in fact he was referring to killing a person.

Rolling "believed in evil spirits" and felt certain that a demon looked out for him "because he had always been lucky in his crimes and he's got away with a lot of things". He mentioned a girl in his hometown who had some of his camping equipment and who "he prays y'all don't never find her." He also discussed yet another escape plan in which prison guards would be disarmed. During the escape, he "wanted as many people killed as possible" and he hoped for a "massacre . . . to drive panic" to give him the best chance of getting away.

Task force investigators also met with Russell Binstead who told detectives that Rolling "looked at himself as being a terrorist" and he "operated best in darkness" because he "loved to instill terror in people." He said that he liked using a knife for killing "because it was a personal weapon . . . something that you got in close with."

~~~~~

In early November 1992, Republican and Alachua County State Attorney Len Register lost his re-election bid to Democrat Rod Smith, who had been endorsed by Alachua County Sheriff Lu Hindrey and Gainesville Police Chief Wayland Clifton. It was the first time in 55 years that there was an election for the state attorney position in Gainesville. Afterward, Register revealed that Chief Clifton had pressured him to arrest Edward Humphrey early in the investigation. Register said that he refused to seek an arrest warrant for Humphrey because insufficient evidence existed despite the fact that the task force had been spending nearly all of its time on him.
~~~~~

"It would have been a miscarriage of justice," Register stated matter-of-factly.

Chapter 19

Fall 1992 – Spring 1993

"Shut off the lights, sweetheart, lock the door, and come to bed. Your woman's waiting for you" (Sondra London letter to Danny Rolling 1/28/93)

As Bobby Lewis spent more time with Danny Rolling, he began to fall under his spell, confiding in a letter to London: *I sure hate the things he has done. But it's sure hard not to like him. I can't help but like him*. He also advised that Rolling was *crazy in love with you*, commenting that Rolling *is more at peace & happy & smiling more than any time I've known him.* In the same letter, he revealed that Rolling *told me the complete story of the woman who's head he cut off. Every detail. It makes a Stephen King book look like a comic book*, and he referred to Rolling as *A Monster of All Time*.

On January 17, 1993, Lewis informed prison officials that Rolling wanted to talk with law enforcement about "past homicides." Rolling would be willing to discuss the Gainesville murders in detail, but only through Lewis, using Lewis as his mouthpiece. He produced a two-page document handwritten by Rolling in which the accused serial killer listed five conditions he wanted met in exchange for "cleaning up this mess" by providing information about the five student murders. The first condition requested that Sondra London be allowed to visit him. Rolling also wanted assurances that he would be kept away from other inmates and get "peace and quiet to do his time for seven months" until he went to Death Row, the "environment he is actually looking for".

In a follow-up interview on January 24, Lewis shared some specifics about the murders. Rolling told him that Christa Hoyt had screamed through the tape covering her mouth when he stabbed her, "sort of kicked for about eight to ten seconds, and then was still." Rolling said she was "extremely beautiful and the best fuck he had ever had in his entire life." At the last crime scene, he had been surprised at how ferociously Manny Taboada had tried to defend himself. Manny had fought "like a wild man," cursing him and struggling until his last breath. Lewis said that Rolling did not seem remorseful about the Gainesville murders. Indeed, he gloated to Lewis that the Ka-bar knife he used for all of the killings was so sharp "it was like cutting butter, even cutting through a couple bones was nothing to it."

Lewis also produced a lengthy handwritten document containing details that Rolling told him about the murders of Christi Powell and Sonja Larson. The document began by describing how in the dark, early morning hours of August 24, clad entirely in black and wearing a black ski mask to boot, Rolling had quietly climbed sixteen wooden steps leading to the back door of Sonja and Christi's apartment. Surprised to find the door unlocked, he slipped into the apartment at 3:00 a.m. and saw Christi Powell asleep on the couch.

> *I stood over her for a moment then crept up the staircase into Sonja Larson's second floor bedroom. She was stabbed several times. The first blow landed in the area of her upper left chest near the collar bone. At the same instant, I pressed a double strip of masking tape over her mouth to muffle her cries. She fought and I stabbed her again. She tried to fend off the blows with her arms. One blow pierced her right upper breast but only nicked it. She continued to struggle so I*

stabbed her again. I'm not sure how many times or where except the last blow was inflicted to the inside of her left thigh. The whole thing lasted nearly 30 seconds and she died.

Then I crept back down stairs and stood over Christina Powell. She had not heard anything and was still asleep on the couch. I then pressed a double strip of tape over her mouth. She put up little resistance. I taped her hands behind her back, stripped her, and raped her. Then led her to the middle of the living room, made her lay down on her stomach, and stabbed her in the back one time through the heart or upper right lung.

Then I went back upstairs and removed the tape from Ms. Larson. She had on panties printed with little animals on them. I think it was teddy bears. I'm not sure but I removed them then spread her legs. I had no sex with her. I only looked.

Then I descended the staircase, pulled the knife from the back of Ms. Christina Powell, removed the tape from her mouth and hands, then douched out her vagina with a cleanser they had in the kitchen. Turned her over on her back and cut off her nipples and moved to the kitchen where I ate an apple and a banana and left taking Ms. Powell's nipples with me in a sandwich bag which were thrown away the next day.

The document included similar accounts of the other three Gainesville murders, including how he raped Tracy Paules once before killing her and then a second time after she was dead. Afterward, he douched out her vagina with a cleanser he found in the apartment, just as he had done to Christi Powell.

~~~~~

Despite learning the lurid details about the depraved acts committed by Rolling, Lewis still felt empathy for him for what he had endured, sympathizing with him for what he had experienced that shaped him into a murderer. In a January 26 letter to Sondra London, Lewis described Rolling as *one of the most tortured, pitiful people I've ever met, capable of the most terrible things I've ever ran into in my criminal career*. He continued to struggle with his feelings about potentially testifying against Rolling: *I have such a conflict of emotions over what he did versus the rest of him and what I know that made him that way*.

~~~~~

Four days later, Lewis provided another written account of the murders committed by Rolling. Purportedly dictated to him by Rolling, the January 30 document detailed the 1989 Grissom family triple-homicide.

One overcast cloudy night in Shreveport, Louisiana around 10:00 p.m., I rode my yellow bike across the field behind the Grissom's home. I left the bike and jumped the fence into their backyard.

Mr. Grissom had been barbequing on his back porch while his grandson Sean Grissom came home.

Mr. Tom Grissom had left the back door open and I burst into the living room. I was wearing camouflage pants, jungle boots, black t-shirt, Kabar knife slung from a makeshift shoulder holster, leather gloves, .38 revolver, and mask.

I commanded that the Grissoms lay on the floor. I then handcuffed Mr. Tom Grissom behind his back and duct taped his mouth closed.

I then went to Ms. Julie Grissom and duct taped her hands behind her back and taped her mouth closed. I then did the same to poor little Sean Grissom.

I then led Mr. Tom Grissom from the living room into the utility room by the washer & dryer and stabbed him twice. First in the right kidney, then the second time below his sternum driving the knife upward into his heart. This was done from behind. I reached over his right shoulder and brought the blade back towards me.

He then returned to the living room where 8-year-old Sean still lay bound and helpless on his stomach. He carefully pulled the tape off of Sean's mouth.

"Sorry to have to do this, kid," Rolling said in a voice only slightly louder than a whisper.

"I'm a man," Sean replied defiantly, his voice firm but wavering.

Rolling hesitated. He looked into the eyes of the terrified boy trying so hard to hide his fear, acting so brave in the face of death. He relaxed the grip on his Ka-Bar knife for a moment. But only for a moment.

"Yes, you are a man," he agreed with a smile expressing sadness.

Then he plunged the knife deep into the boy's back. He watched with troubled eyes as the flame of life faded away and snuffed out entirely in "less than six seconds." Although he died quickly, the boy's look of terrified disbelief remained frozen on his face long after the moment of his death.

The handwritten narrative continued its recitation of the grisly details in Rolling's own words:

> *I then led Ms. Julie Grissom into Mr. Tom Grissom's bedroom and undressed her. She was wearing long leather boots, panty hose, tan lace bra, white blouse, and a shirt.*
>
> *I then led her into the bathroom and raped her on the sink counter top then placed her in the bath tub and washed her vagina. Then douched her out with the shower head.*

I then led her back into Mr. Tom Grissom's bedroom, forced her to lay on the bed face down, and stabbed her 3 times in the back once on the right side once on the left side and once over the spine. She died in less than 10 seconds and it was over.

I then pulled her body to the other side of the bed, removed the tape, spread her legs, went to the kitchen and got some vinegar and douched her out again and left her body that way, spread eagle on the edge of the bed near the pillow at the head of the bed.

I then returned to the utility room with some clothing items and placed them in the washer and washed it. I then removed the tape and handcuffs from Mr. Grissom leaving him face down in a pool of blood on the floor. I then returned to young Sean and removed the tape from him and left the scene.

Rolling's chilling account of the cold-blooded killings included directions to where he disposed of the murder weapon as well as the .38 revolver he subsequently used to shoot his father, James. He claimed to have thrown both weapons into a small pond behind a junior high school in Shreveport. A hand-drawn map detailed the layout of the location. According to Lewis, the only regret Rolling expressed about the Shreveport murders was that he "hated killing the kid."

By January 31, Lewis had heard so much about Rolling's violent acts and history of "tremendous personality changes" that he began to worry about his own safety.

"I ain't no real big coward," he told the investigators, but Rolling "half scares me to fucking death. This guy sits there and explains to me how he kills people in their sleep, in detail . . . and explains to me the people he's killed that he feels like has betrayed him."

Fortunately for Lewis, Rolling decided the time had come for him to meet with the task force investigators face to face. He signed a waiver of rights on January 31 and appended it with a handwritten withdrawal of his previous invocation of counsel. At 8:25 that night, he met with detectives and confirmed his willingness to discuss the murders but, wanting to have some control over the situation, he reasserted that he would only do so through Bobby Lewis, his "mouthpiece" and "confessor."

"I'm not discussing anything about the Gainesville murders to you gentlemen other than through Bobby," he told them calmly. "Y'all want to know something – talk to him . . . Ask him a question and he'll ask me – I'll tell him, he'll tell you."

He wanted to come clean about the killings and clear everything up, but he also wanted to help Lewis in the process. Rolling felt like he owed him something.

"When I was brought here and put on W-Wing, the guards used to come to my cell and threaten me daily . . . and the only person that showed me any kind of decency was Bobby," Rolling explained. "And that, for a man in my shoes, that means more than gold."

After discussing the parameters of the interview with FDLE Agent Ed Dix and Detective Sgt. Legran Hewitt of the Alachua County Sheriff's Office, and after reconfirming Rolling's waiver of rights, Detective Steve Kramig of the

Gainesville Police Department began the questioning. The process did not go smoothly at first.

> SK: Okay, here we go, I'm going to ask you a question. Danny, did you kill the two girls at Williamsburg?
>
> DR: No, I'm not going to answer any of your questions concerning any of that. There's the man you need to speak to right there (indicating Lewis).
>
> ED: He knows the answer to that?
>
> DR: Are y'all going to ask me this again? I told you Bobby is my mouthpiece. He is my confessor. I have confessed to him. He will speak to you.
>
> BL: I'm free to give y'all any answer y'all want concerning all five murders in Gainesville and the whereabouts of the murder weapons.
>
> . . . . .
>
> SK: All right, you said I could ask you questions.
>
> DR: No, gentlemen. I said you could talk to Bobby. And y'all are speaking to me.
>
> . . . . .
>
> SK: About these homicides, you don't want to talk to us about the homicides. You want us to

ask him the questions, is that correct?

DR: That's what we discussed the minute I came in here.

SK: It's not workable.

ED: Danny, let me ask you this. If we get the information from Bobby and we want to clarify something, can you clarify it for us?

DR: I'm not going to add two cents to this.

SK: It's not a workable situation, Ed, end the tape.

ED: Okay, we'll terminate the interview at 9:35 p.m.

After some additional discussion and clarification, the interview resumed fifteen minutes later.

LH: On August 26th of 1990 there was two bodies found at Williamsburg Apartments in Gainesville, Florida . . . Was Danny Rolling responsible for those homicides?

BL: Yes, he was.

LH: Is that correct, Danny?

DR: Yes, sir.

The questioning followed in that format the rest of the way. The detectives would ask Lewis a question relating to the murders and Lewis would provide an answer, then they would ask Rolling if what Lewis had just answered was accurate, and Rolling would confirm it or occasionally clarify by adding some detail. When the questioning was done, he had confessed to all five of the Gainesville murders.

After killing his final victim, Tracy Paules, Rolling disposed of the knife and gloves used for the crimes because he had "decided to quit what he was doing . . . that was to be the last victim." He buried them in an old wooden chicken coop not far from the Gator Inn. Before going back to his camp, he cleaned himself off in the pool of a nearby apartment complex, the clear water turning dirty red as he washed off the blood of his victims with a solitary nighttime swim.

Lewis told the investigators that Rolling felt compelled to commit the crimes by an uncontrollable force, an irresistible urging that took over his body and mind.

> Danny breaks himself down into different personalities that are the driving force behind what Danny does. There's "Danny," there's a "Jesse James" sort of side of Danny, there is a force that comes out of Danny known as "Ynnad," there's a force that comes out of Danny known as "Gemini". Gemini was who you would have found at the five murder scenes.

He also believed that supernatural forces guided his actions, telling the detectives that "there really is demons" and "forces in this world that can overpower even the strongest of us. I've seen 'em and I know it's real just as sure as there's angels in Heaven and there's devils in Hell."

Rolling repeatedly insisted that he had not sodomized any of his victims, although the evidence at the Tracy Paules murder scene said otherwise. While adamant that he did not hate his father, Rolling emphasized that, while growing up, the environment at home "was constantly in turmoil"

> [I]t was a roller coaster ride, you know. Mom and Dad would fight so bad. You know, Dad drove my Mom to the point she had a . . . massive nervous breakdown, complete nervous breakdown. But Dad couldn't help the way he was. I don't know why he was the way he was. And so I would use that other as sort of like an escape. I would look and see how other people were living and how they were happy, and I would like to sort of become a member of their family in a way.

On February 4, Rolling met with the task force detectives again, amazed that they had been unable to locate the Ka-Bar knife he used to kill the Gainesville students, even though he had told them specifically where he buried it. He also talked about his different personalities.

> I have dealt with different personalities all my life but they really became prevalent in my life when I was in solitary confinement in Parchman Penitentiary in a cell that got flooded out once and twice, sometimes three times a week, with about three inches of raw sewage. And I just kind of like, well, they became a reality to me more so than ever before. But the person that I really have struggled against to prevent becoming . . . is a person called Gemini who is, um, he is evil, period.

. . . . .

I wouldn't want anybody to
be me.

The next day, Sondra London drove to Florida State Prison to meet Rolling in person for the first time. They met in a small carrel of the prison's visiting room. A cloudy Plexiglas divider separated them as they talked for nearly two hours. Throughout the visit, a prison guard sat behind Rolling, observing and taking notes.

"It's been really hard trying to get in here to see you," London told Rolling.

"Well, that's all over now because we're cooperating with the State," Rolling replied.

London did not know who Rolling meant by "we" or what he called "cooperating."

"What does Rick Parker think about all of this?" she asked.

"Who?"

"Rick Parker, your lawyer."

"Oh, him? I don't care what he thinks. I've made up my mind about what I'm going to do, and if he doesn't like it, I'll just fire him."

Rolling paused to observe her reaction.

"We are cooperating with the State, and I want you to know that I'm doing this so that we can be together," he declared. "I'm doing this for us."

Nothing was mentioned about the murders; however, Rolling gave her his blessing to release a statement to the media, as well as any songs, art, or other items he had given her.

"Run with it, babe," he told her.

When their time was up, they pressed their hands against the Plexiglas, unable to touch, but sharing a connection nonetheless.

"I'll be back," London assured him.

The following Monday, February 8, London sent an announcement to various media outlets in the form of a press release:

> *On Friday, February 5, I had an exclusive personal interview with accused serial killer DANNY HAROLD ROLLING, the mysterious singing drifter who is awaiting trial on five murder and three rape charges in the 1990 mutilation slayings of five college students in Gainesville, Florida.*
>
> *ROLLING, 38, requested this interview in order to announce his intention to talk with the State's investigators about his case, under the sole condition that he be allowed the privilege of having me visit him as his personal friend and confidante for the duration of his ordeal.*
>
> *By EXCLUSIVE agreement and upon his request, all of ROLLING's forthcoming statements will be released by me PERSONALLY.*
>
> *Extensive background material on DANNY ROLLING has been copyrighted and is now*

available for publication, including EXCLUSIVE original stories, photos, artwork and songs.

She did not realize that Rolling had already been providing details about the murders to investigators. Nonetheless, Department of Corrections officials were not amused by London's announcement. They immediately fired off a letter informing her that, based on the "misrepresentation" as to the nature of her approved "social visit" on February 5, she would no longer be allowed to visit Rolling at Florida State Prison.

Spurred on by what he perceived to be deliberate mistreatment of his love interest, and perhaps prompted by some misguided notion of chivalry, on February 15, Rolling arranged an interview with Kathy Belich, a reporter from Orlando-based Channel 9 news station WFTV. Wearing a blue prison jumpsuit with deputies and lawyers seated beside and behind him, Rolling read a three-minute prepared statement in a soft-spoken, Southern drawl. He began by asserting Sondra London to be "of the highest caliber, sincere and honest, a woman of extraordinary talents," and then scolded the media, proclaiming "it's a shame the way the media has bashed her of late." He also announced that all future communications from members of the media should go through London, who would henceforth be acting as his personal representative and spokesperson.

~~~~~

London subsequently posted a video of the "interview" on YouTube. Years later, "Saphire Blue" commented:

He did seem to have a certain amount of guilt. Some killers seem to have no conscious, [sic] and never regret what they do. Others, like Rolling, seem to have guilt, but have an urge they
~~~~~

cannot control. That is not the same as a sociopath . . . . The mind of Danny Rolling is the most interesting of all the serial killers.

And another poster wrote:

My heart aches for the little boy who was so severely abused emotionally and mentally by his father. His entire life was heartbreaking. I hate it that he couldn't find a way to be healed of those wounds before he wounded others. A life full of tragedy all the way around. May he rest in peace and his abusive father be held accountable. I have no sympathy for the serial killer but I do for the unloved abused boy.

~~~~~

On February 19, Bobby Lewis told the *Gainesville Sun* newspaper that Rolling stalked his Gainesville victims "to some degree" before killing them.

"There's a lot of people who just don't realize how lucky they were over there," Lewis said cryptically. "One little minor thing or another made him on one particular night or another turn away from your window or door."

Lewis claimed that Rolling asked him to talk to investigators about the murders on his behalf because he could not bear to discuss the details of the crimes himself.

"He said, "'Look, you know I'm guilty. I can't live like this. I've got to get right with God. I need to get this out. The things I've done are so horrible and so terrible,'" Lewis recounted.
~~~~~

Around the same time, Sondra London wrote a lengthy letter to Rolling discussing prison officials' continuing denials of her requests to visit him. Before concluding the letter, she proposed a solution to the problem:

> *I've been in love before, but it was never like this . . . The first kind of love I felt was maternal – I loved little Danny – I wanted to make him my own CHILD – where he could grow & be all that was in him to become. I wanted to shield him & protect him & play with him. Then came the thrill of the creative interplay. Knowing you has lit a fire in the artist in me that is burning higher & higher -- & I LOVE that feeling! Don't you? I know you feel exactly the same way – inspired. Slowly, I began to see you as "200 lbs of HARD MAN" & that was another kind of love. That's the one that became so dizzying when I finally laid eyes on my gorgeous hunk of masculinity . . . And to be told I will never see you again – this is tearing me up. Darling, I wonder . . . would you like to get MARRIED?*

On February 25, just a few days after mailing the letter, London received a letter from Rolling mirroring her marriage proposal. The two marriage proposals had crossed in the mail. They now considered themselves to be engaged. The jailhouse romance instantly attracted more media attention to the case.

Two weeks later, Rolling and London appeared on the tabloid TV show, *A Current Affair*. In addition to professing their love for each other, Rolling sang a gospel song and described his execution day as a time when the "glory and the peace and the love of it all will be waiting for me." A few weeks later, *Geraldo* aired an episode featuring London and her relationship with Rolling. The show's host, Geraldo Rivera, called London "strange and fascinating" and showed a Valentine's Day card Rolling made for her with the handwritten message: "You can run, but you can't hide. Hold on tight, you're in for a hell of a ride."

Bobby Lewis wrote to London on March 26, clearly frustrated by the fact that she was letting her feelings for Rolling cloud her judgment.

> *You're in love with a fantasy, an image, not a person. You've never been alone with him 5 minutes -- and you would not stay with him a week. I know you, I know him, and that's the truth. You have turned yourself into some type of criminal groupie, and it's very self-destructive.*
>
> . . . . .
>
> *As to Danny, he will be found guilty. They have tons of evidence. He will get 5 death sentences. He will go to death row. All this is fact . . . I will not at all be surprised if he don't take his own life some day . . . you do not know the man at all that you love – I do.*
>
> . . . . .
>
> *You totally destroyed your big story – a chance at credibility,*

> *a real future . . . you destroyed your credibility with the "I love him".*

Upset about his inability to have visitations with London, Rolling filed an Inmate Grievance bemoaning the denial of his "right to marry the woman I love" and asserting that "we only want to marry & visit each other quietly once a week. Is that too much to ask?" A terse response denied his request on the ground that London "indicated that she is interested in profiting from the circumstances that you are presently in."

~~~~~

On April 10, Edward Humphrey celebrated his 21st birthday in an upscale Orlando restaurant with his publicist along with a photographer and reporter from the *Orlando Sentinel* newspaper. Wearing a polo shirt, tan pants, and sunglasses, Humphrey hesitated when the waiter brought him a large knife to cut his birthday cake.

"Don't take a picture of me with the knife," he said only half-joking. "That's all I need."

The experience of being hounded by the media and persecuted as a murderer in the eyes of the public had permanently jaded his perspective on the press, police, and the courts. He became much more conscious of his appearance, much more careful with his words, much less trusting. As a result of what he experienced, he lived with a paralyzing level of self-consciousness most never have the burden of carrying.

"I don't want people to read about me," he told the reporter under the watchful gaze of his publicist. "I don't want people to know who I am. I mean, it's just a really bad feeling – knowing that wherever you go people are judging you, and they don't even know you. They've never even talked to you. But people do it to me all the time."
~~~~~

He eyed the reporter warily. Though no longer named the prime suspect in perhaps the biggest manhunt in state history, he also had not been eliminated as a person of interest either. And the notoriety had not diminished following his release from prison. After being released on parole, he had tried and tried to find a job, only to be rejected again and again. No one wanted to hire an accused killer, let alone someone suspected of brutally murdering five people. Humphrey told the reporter how one grocery store clerk had called him at home after yet another rejection.

"I feel really bad about this," the clerk told him, "but they knew who you were, and when you left they were all laughing and saying, 'Man, we're not going to give *that guy* a job.'"

His only job prospect came from his court-ordered 62 hours of community service at the local Humane Society, which liked his work enough to hire him afterward.

"I'm just like anybody else," he said. "I've got feelings, too, and that stuff really hurt me. I'll never, ever get over it completely. And I'll never be able to forget it."

Chapter 20

September 1993 – February 1994

Pretrial Discovery

"*Thus the struggle begins, Good and Evil within*" (Danny Rolling)

On September 15, 1993, Sondra London wrote Rolling about his upcoming resentencing hearing:

> *I wouldn't miss your court appearance for the world. And you may be sure every major news outlet will be there as well. I don't know if I will get to touch you or kiss you or even whisper in your ear, but your lawyer will ask the judge for that privilege. If we are very very lucky, we will get some contact. If only it could be PRIVATE! But I'm afraid that's beyond my wildest dreams at this point . . . .*
>
> *If it was up to the Maniac in me, I would throw you down, rip your clothes right off and rape you QUICK! But I will have to keep the Maniac in the Box, and let the Perfect Lady have the honors of standing by MY DANNY. I'll just have to rape you silently with my eyes.*

She promised that the "inside" story about him remained confidential:

Nobody here knows anything about MISTER MYSTERY. And that's the way I intend to keep it. Everything I know about you is going to be released in MY BOOK. I'm not jabbering my head off about you to reporters.

But London also chastised him for not telling her about a pen-pal relationship he had developed with another female writer:

Were you deliberately hiding this from me? Did you think I would not find out? Did you think that when I did find out it would not bother me? If you are STILL concealing any more so-called "relationships" or correspondence of that kind at all with ANYONE but your FAMILY and ME, I want you to reveal that to me NOW . . . Because if you DON'T I can PROMISE you it will come out later . . . I have my limits on how far I will let ANY MAN take advantage of me. Danny Rolling or not, I have to maintain my own self-respect.

. . . . .

You swear you're all mine, but you were swearing the same thing the whole time you were writing to her. And you were swearing the same thing when you gave Kathy Belich an EXCLUSIVE interview.

Later in the same letter, she mocked the efforts of the task force investigators:

> *I'm looking at this story, and I'm thinking, it's almost like that drowning I witnessed, where they had this big organized search effort going on that looked great, but meanwhile the sea gave up the victim when it got good & ready. Sure, the body was found, but rescuers weren't responsible. It's like that with the Gainesville Murders. All these cops falling all over each other, all those millions of dollars spent . . . but when they found the guy they finally charged, it turns out they had him all along and were too DUMB to know it.*
>
> *So where's your Hero Cops? Every crime story's gotta have one, so who's the Hero in the Cop Shop?*

~~~~~

On September 23, London appeared at the Alachua County State Attorney's Office in Gainesville for her deposition. London told prosecution and defense attorneys that she first met Rolling through Bobby Lewis who had shown Rolling the manuscript she wrote about Lewis called "Red Bone." She said that Rolling had been so impressed with her writing ability that he contacted her by letter asking if she wanted to write his story.

London testified that she no longer had any type of relationship with Lewis because he "set Danny up and wants him dead." According to London, Lewis became upset when she became a "glory hog" and started getting more media
~~~~~

attention than him because he had wanted the story to be "about Bobby, the hero, who saves the day and solves the mystery and catches the terrible killer, Danny."

She tried to explain how she had grown to love Rolling despite her intention of maintaining an emotional distance from him.

> The development of my feelings for Danny is kind of a sensitive issue. I would have to say this . . . my feelings developed gradually, and during the whole process, I resisted any emotional warmth that I was feeling. I attempted to deny it to myself and to anyone else . . . It was sort of a conflict there within me because I did not want to fall in love with him.

She expressed disdain for Rolling's other female admirers and pen pals, particularly "petite brunette reporters" such as Lynn Hooper of the *Orlando Sentinel* and Jaine Abdo, a UF student and reporter for the student-run newspaper, *The Independent Alligator*. With venom in her voice, London railed against them for "trying to come between me and my big story and my man, both at once." She had even gone to Abdo's office to confront her in an effort to protect her investment in the "biggest story that's hit Florida ever." In addition to standing by her love for Rolling, London viewed herself as the "only one who can unlock [his] secrets." She stressed that her motivation was not fame or fortune, but rather to be "of assistance to the people of the State of Florida in uncovering the secrets that are within the mind of Danny Rolling, and that no one else has access to." She also asserted that Rolling never made any admissions or statements to her about the Gainesville homicides.

"I don't care anything about the prosecution, the defense, the murder, nothing. All I care about is having my hands on Danny Rolling."

On September 27, Rolling attended a resentencing hearing on his conviction for robbing the Ocala Winn-Dixie. Necessitated after his original sentence was overturned because he had not been told that he faced a life sentence as a habitual offender before entering his plea of guilty, the resentencing hearing took place in the Marion County Jail due to the need for increased security precautions. Keenly aware that Sondra London planned to attend the proceeding, authorities worried that she might try to aid Rolling in an escape attempt.

During the hearing, Judge Thomas Sawaya asked Rolling if he had anything he wished to say. Rolling looked over at Sondra London, seated on a bench in the area set aside for the public.

"Sondra, they might keep you from me," he exclaimed, "but I want you to know they can't stamp out the love and affection that I have for you in my heart."

Then he began to sing: "I recall the day I first saw you. I reached out to say that I love you." His serenade went on for several minutes, culminating with "Tell me baby, what were my words, all my tears run together, baby, just like rain," before Judge Sawaya silenced him and resentenced him to life in prison.

London no doubt felt flattered by Rolling's serenade, writing him in a subsequent letter: *I talked to a reporter the other day who was in court when you sang. She couldn't get over it. She said you reminded her of ELVIS. Early Elvis. She said the same thing most people say when they look at your artwork: "What a WASTE!*

~~~~~

As the pretrial discovery process began in earnest, the attorneys for the prosecution and defense took the
~~~~~

depositions of witness after witness, hoping to gain some nugget of information that would give them an edge at trial. On October 15, Bernadine Holder appeared for her deposition at the Caddo Parish Courthouse in Shreveport. Mrs. Holder had known the Rolling family for nearly thirty years and lived directly across the street from them. She said that Danny "always got along with everybody" and "everybody liked" him. Although she considered Claudia Rolling to be a close friend and frequently visited her in the Rolling home, Mrs. Holder did not have such fond memories of James Rolling.

She described James as a "very weird man" and a "nut" who "tried to intimidate anybody around him." He "didn't believe in love" and told her that "there's no such thing as love" because "if somebody loves you, they use you, they want something from you."

Mrs. Holder also recalled how James often "dehumanized" and abused Claudia and his sons, especially Danny, who he "physically and emotionally abused every day of his life." She testified about one occasion when James, wearing his Shreveport Police uniform, beat Danny in the front yard with his fists. James beat Danny, who was around 14 years old at the time, "in his head and in the back," kicking and hitting him until Danny fell to the ground "and then he still beat him."

According to Mrs. Holder, when James found out about Danny's arrest for the Gainesville murders, he did not react like one would expect a concerned father to react. Instead, he seemed happy.

"Danny's going to get the electric chair and he's going to fry," James told her. "I'll be glad to see him fry. He deserves it."

The next day, Danny's former wife, Omatha Lummus, testified at deposition in Bossier City, Louisiana. She had met Danny through the United Pentecostal Church of Shreveport, which they both attended. After a six-month courtship, the 19-year-old "was pretty sure" that she loved

Rolling, and they got married on September 6, 1974, in the church.

Throughout the time they dated, Danny treated her with tenderness and seemed serious about the church and his Bible studies. But that all changed after Omatha became pregnant. No longer the warm, caring man that he had been, Danny began disappearing from the house without a word of warning, sometimes for hours, sometimes for days. Once he did not come back for two weeks. Omatha found out later that he was doing drugs many of the times he went missing. One night during Danny's latest vanishing act, two police officers appeared at the front door. Danny had been caught peeping into women's windows.

"It was embarrassing," Omatha said, "humiliating."

In March 1976, their daughter, Kiley, was born. Although at times Danny seemed happy being a father, his actions and attitude were inconsistent, and he kept disappearing for periods of time. Omatha eventually decided to confront him about his drug use, but Danny did not like her trying to lay down the law, and the confrontation left her with a swollen, black eye. Another argument, in which Danny pointed a shotgun at her and threatened to kill her, convinced Omatha to leave him. She took Kiley and never went back.

~~~~~

Rolling's first cousin, Charles Strozier, appeared for deposition in Shreveport on October 13. Beginning when he was 6 years old, Strozier had frequent contact with Rolling and his family. The two boys played together two or three times a week, and as they got older, Strozier noticed how strangely Rolling's father acted.

"He was unpredictable. You didn't know what mood he was going to be in. He can be in a good mood where he would pat you on the back and want to talk to you [but] there
~~~~~

would be other times where he would cut your throat, if he could."

Strozier "was always afraid of James" and described him as treating Danny "like an animal." He recalled how Rolling's father frequently beat them across the stomach with a belt and that if Rolling or his brother cried they would get beat more severely because "James Harold didn't like weakness." Even family meals were stressful events that James made "like eating in a boot camp." No one could talk unless he directly asked them a question.

Strozier described Rolling as a "loner" during high school whose only interests seemed to be playing guitar, drawing, and writing songs. Yet, like Bernadine Holder, he also described Danny as "a real easy-going kind of person" who "got along with everybody."

Danny's brother, Kevin, gave his deposition at the same place about a month later. Kevin did not recall specific instances of abuse by their father, but he acknowledged that "him and Danny didn't get along" and admitted that he might have blocked out certain memories:

> I don't remember Danny ever being whipped by my father, I don't remember any of that. People tell me it happened and I don't know. I don't have a glimmer of it.
>
> . . . . .
>
> I'm not saying this stuff didn't happen. What I'm telling you is I don't have any memory of it. There's a bunch of things I don't remember. Great big gaping holes in my memory.

Asked to explain why he thought Danny had committed so many crimes during his life, Kevin sat quietly with a furrowed brow. After some time he answered that Danny "don't think about nothing, he just goes through life a moment at a time" and "never seemed to grow up."

~~~~~

On January 6, 1994, the First District Court of Appeal reversed the trial court order prohibiting the disbursement of proceeds Sondra London obtained from Rolling's stories, artwork, and other items. As grounds for the reversal, the appellate court ruled that the order improperly attempted to control the proceeds relating to "all crimes," including those for which Rolling had not yet been convicted.

Two weeks later, on the morning of January 20, forensic psychiatrist Robert Sadoff testified at deposition about his psychological examination of Rolling. His first examination occurred in November 1993, and he quickly diagnosed Rolling with borderline personality disorder, while also finding him to be an obsessive-compulsive person who is "very clean, and very neat, and very orderly."

Sadoff revealed that the initial examination session had not gone smoothly. Several hours into it, while questioning Rolling about the Gainesville homicides, he noticed Rolling sweating and getting "very agitated and very nervous" that his Gemini personality would come out. At one point, Rolling put his head down.

"I can't do it," he said wearily. "Don't – don't ask me about that now. I'm afraid. *He's* going to be here. It's him. I can't – I can't be sure he won't come out."

Wary of the possibility of facing a homicidal personality, Sadoff decided to end the examination. As Sadoff recounted, "I wasn't that curious about seeing Gemini in an unprotected situation, in the event that he was pure evil, as Danny has referred to him."

Asked if Gemini could be a fabrication, an attempt by Rolling to build-up an insanity defense, Dr. Sadoff replied to the contrary.
~~~~~

> I think that Danny -- who has a very strict religious background, who believes in Heaven and Hell, who believes in devils and angels, and believed . . . that he made this deal with Gemini at Parchman Prison – and believed there was such an evil spirit. He believed it profoundly, and he believed that he gave his soul up to Gemini and had no control.

Sadoff testified that Rolling truly felt remorse about what he had done and that he feared his Gemini side, "which means he's afraid of that evil part of himself and wants to keep the lid on it." Pressed to elaborate whether Rolling had "control of that evil part of himself," he answered by expanding the question.

"It's my opinion that most of us have a lot of control over it," he replied, "but there are times, under the right circumstances, when anybody, pushed to the limit, could let himself or herself lose control and do something violent."

According to Sadoff, the eclipse of Rolling's good side by his evil side involved a process of gradual escalation beginning with voyeurism as a coping mechanism for getting away from the pressures of his overbearing and abusive father at home.

> Danny doesn't start out killing and raping. He starts out with voyeurism. Voyeurism is the intrusion, by vision, into somebody else's privacy. Where does he go from there? He breaks into places. He robs. He burglarizes. Then he rapes; doesn't kill first, just rapes. That's an intrusion into

> someone's privacy. And then, once he has done that, he goes further.
>
> . . . . .
>
> The voyeur is intruding himself, without permission, into your privacy, and I think that is often the beginning of people who then intrude themselves in a more offensive way, such as burglarizing, breaking in, and then raping. With a rape there is an assault to the privacy of the individual. And then, finally, the ultimate is the rape-murder, where there is the stabbing or the intrusion into the body of the person, not into an already made orifice, but you're creating your own orifice, so to speak.

According to Dr. Sadoff, Rolling admitted to having committed five rapes without killing, including women in Savannah and Sarasota, before he began murdering his rape victims. The need to kill began in Parchman Prison with his "deal with the Devil."

Sadoff found the extent to which Rolling mutilated some of his victims astonishing. He emphasized that while an angry person might kill by stabbing over and over again, Rolling's deliberate positioning of the bodies and the "cutting and mutilation" revealed a "very disturbed mind, a very, very sick, disturbed degree of psychopathology." In his thirty years of experience, which included some "very serious and very significant killings," Sadoff had "never seen anything like that before."

> I've seen people who have killed in a serial fashion. I have

> seen people who are mass murderers, who have killed all at once. I have seen people who have raped, and who have stabbed, and who have shot.
>
> I have never seen anything like the bizarreness of the photographs that I saw for these five, and especially the third one of Christa Hoyt, ever. I don't think anybody else has either.

~~~~~

Rolling's attorney, Richard Parker, set Edward Humphrey's deposition for February 2 in the Orlando office of his attorney, Donald Lykkebak. Humphrey could not recall anything that he had said during the overnight interrogation by FDLE agents after his arrest. He remembered only that the agents had kept him awake for 30 hours and ignored his requests for his manic-depressive medication. He also denied knowing Rolling or ever having met or even seen him in person, and likewise denied knowing or ever meeting any of the five murdered Gainesville students.

~~~~~

Depositions of the parties' medical experts continued on February 4 with clinical psychologist Elizabeth McMahon. Dr. McMahon rejected the notion that Rolling had suffered any brain damage in his past that would affect his behavior. Instead, she believed that he lacked emotional maturity, the roots of which could be traced back to his childhood and conflicting emotions about his parents. He loved his mother, but at the same time resented her for "her abandonment of her two boys to the abuse of the father." Rolling also had mixed feelings about his father.

"He's very, very ambivalent about his father," she expounded. "He's angry, but he loves him," a "childish love of trying to get his approval," rather than a healthy, mature one.

Dr. McMahon described Rolling as being unable to regulate his emotions and lacking the internal ability to control his reactions to external events.

"He will go from angry to calm, to sad, to nice, to cordial, to pissed," she explained. "His feelings of affect is on a roller coaster, and it changes very rapidly."

She diagnosed Rolling with borderline personality disorder due to his lack of emotional development.

"We're talking about somebody who is eight or nine [years old] on a bright day, on his brightest day," she asserted. "He's fine intellectually. But we're talking about somebody who has the emotional development of a child."

As a borderline, Rolling could not understand or care about the feelings of another human being. Though he himself lacked an essential sense of self, he split everyone else into categories -- good or bad -- and could change anyone's categorization in an instant for no apparent reason. Ironically, his inability to experience empathy doomed his relationships with others, always causing him to be shocked when the relationships failed since he had no idea about how cruel and uncaring he could be.

McMahon also diagnosed him with the dissociative feature of possession syndrome, stemming from his belief that different personalities possessed and controlled him at various times.

> In the case of the homicides . . . this does not match with Danny's image of himself. In spite of the fact that he's done this, and he knows he's done it, it doesn't match with

> his image of himself. You ask him to describe himself. He's kind, he's loving, he's considerate, you know, he thinks people are wonderful, he says that he's close to God. He's a lot of other things. That's how he sees himself.
>
> So he doesn't see himself as somebody who goes out and rapes and kills. So it's not that his hands . . . are detached from his body, okay? It's that his observing ego is sort of like back here, watching it happen, but you're standing back here, like you're standing behind yourself . . . like people often say, "It's like I'm watching a movie."

The part of Rolling's personality that he dissociated sprang from an "unbelievable rage that he just cannot accept," which "gets expressed in a very eruptive, explosive manner. With Danny, it's a cold rage. It's a rage that is calculated, in the sense that it doesn't erupt in that same fashion. Not that it isn't disruptive, but it doesn't erupt."

Dr. McMahon explained Rolling's antisocial, narcissistic, and dependent features by referencing his history of peeping in windows.

> It had two meanings to him that kept drawing him back. One, of course, is the sexual. He doesn't deny that, but it was much more than that. It was a participation in the life of the family he was watching.

> And he would watch a family consistently for long periods of times . . . not when anything sexual was going on . . . [H]e talks about getting out of bed before dawn . . . when it's a cold and maybe even snowy type of morning, I mean really uncomfortable outside, to stand outside a family's window and simply watch them getting ready to go to work, to leave the house, all the family stuff that was going on, eat breakfast, you know, interact.

This extended period of peeping allowed him to feel a part of whatever family he happened to be watching. McMahon noted that he had engaged in such an extended observation of the Grissom family, watching them for "quite a while," so much so that he "knew the family pattern." Being fired from the restaurant he worked at, for reasons he deemed unjust, tapped into his preexisting, ever-present, deep-seated rage, "and he took it out on the Grissoms."

Along with the abuse by his father and the torments of Parchman Prison, McMahon pointed to Rolling's divorce as a significant contributing cause of his subsequent criminal behavior. As a borderline personality, he would have wanted to avoid "aloneness, or abandonment, or solitary anything, so his wife having left him would have been devastating to him," even though he had caused her to leave in the first place. Indeed, members of his family confirmed that he was "never the same after Omatha left him."

Discussing the murders, McMahon opined that Rolling had posed Christa Hoyt's body and positioned her severed head -- so that it would be the first thing police saw when entering the room -- to spite his father, a former police officer. McMahon also insisted that Rolling could have avoided punishment for the murders, but instead allowed himself to be caught.

> There's absolutely no reason for Danny to have been charged with these homicides, if he hadn't chosen to get himself picked up. If Danny had got on a bus and left the State of Florida, and were today in Seattle, we wouldn't know who did this.
>
> We only know because [he's] sitting in the Ocala jail and starts mouthing and somebody gets him matched . . . he went out of his way to get himself picked up.

On February 8, it was clinical psychologist Harry Krop's turn. Early in his deposition, Dr. Krop explained how he had become involved with Rolling's case. He had received a phone call on January 20, 1991 from Trish Jenkins, a Marion County assistant public defender, who told him that she had a client who was arrested for the armed robbery of an Ocala Winn-Dixie. She said that after meeting the client and reviewing his file, she believed he might have significant mental health problems. She asked Krop to come to Ocala and evaluate him to assess whether he could competently enter into a guilty plea. Krop drove to the Marion County Jail the next day where Jenkins introduced him to her client, Danny Rolling.

In a small office in the jail, the two men discussed the robbery for nearly four hours. Throughout the discussions, Krop noticed that Rolling seemed anxious and constantly picked at scabs that were spread around his body. To put him at ease, Krop assured Rolling that their conversation would remain confidential. By the time Krop finished his questions, he felt confident in deeming Rolling competent to either stand trial or enter a plea on the robbery charges. As Krop started packing up his things to leave, Rolling beckoned him to stay.

"Can we talk about crimes other than the robbery?" Rolling asked.

"Sure, if you want to," Krop replied, concealing his surprise.

"Would what we talk about be confidential? Like the robbery stuff?"

"Yes, everything we talk about is confidential, unless what you say represents a future threat," Krop affirmed.

For the next three hours, Krop listened with fascination and horror as Rolling recounted the details of the Gainesville murders. Afterward, Krop struggled with what to do with the information. His first impulse had been to inform the police about the identity of the Gainesville Ripper, but the confidentiality privilege of the doctor-patient relationship ethically precluded him from doing so. Keeping the secret to himself had been a heavy burden. It tore at him, not just professionally, but on a personal level as well. He could not even comfort his own daughter that the serial student slayer was safely behind bars.

Krop also testified about his interview of James Rolling that took place several weeks earlier in Shreveport. He said that James had a "very strong need to control the structure of the interview, to talk about what he wanted to talk about, and not talk about other things." James blamed Danny's problems on his wife's side of the family, and Krop opined that his failure to acknowledge that any abuse occurred in the Rolling home "reflects the kind of person that Danny describes him as," particularly since he had to know that his denial could increase the likelihood of Danny being sentenced to death.

James Rolling's version of the incident in which Danny shot him differed from Danny's version in that James insisted that he had merely discharged his gun into the air, firing three times into the sky as a warning. He had not aimed at Danny as he fled from the house.

"Why did you shoot in the air?" Krop asked him.

"I learned that in the military," the elder Rolling replied, "because that's a warning, to shoot up in the air. And then I went back in the house and locked the door."

According to James, after he went back into the house, Danny kicked in the door and shot him in the back.

James also described a cycle of abuse that began with his father's treatment of him, which included what Krop called "pretty severe physical abuse" involving belts. He revealed that both of his uncles were schizophrenic, his wife's side of the family had psychiatric problems, and his sister had two sons who had mental problems as well. Dr. Krop opined that this family history of mental illness considerably increased the likelihood that Danny would suffer from a mental disorder, too.

Krop also noted that rather than accepting any responsibility for how Danny turned out, his father placed all of the blame on Danny himself.

"Danny has always lived in a Disney world," James explained. "He's always been a dreamer. He never thinks of the future. He just lives day to day." Later, he added, "I always felt that Danny had mental problems. I can't understand it. He had it made. He just didn't take advantage of what I gave him."

James also sent Krop a rambling letter containing a laundry list of all of the things he claimed to have done to support Danny while he was growing up.

Neither Danny or Kevin had to work outside home growing up. Why? His father.

Who taught them to swim? His father.

Who bought them the best musical instruments? His father.

Never been a Christmas they didn't receive something.

Who fed, housed Danny no cost to Danny? His father.

His father believes the man of the family is the head of the family, no matter what anybody says he won't change.

Did anybody ever stop long enough to say thanks to that man?

Based on his review of the case, Dr. Krop opined that James Rolling's treatment of his son, and the overall dysfunctional family environment that Danny experienced while growing up, significantly increased the probability that he would become a dysfunctional adult. Like Sadoff, Dr. Krop ultimately diagnosed Rolling as suffering from borderline personality disorder.

On the afternoon of February 11, 1994, just a few days before Rolling's trial, clinical psychologist Elizabeth McMahon appeared for another deposition. After examining Rolling in August, October, and November 1993, McMahon diagnosed him as borderline personality disorder with features of antisocial personality, narcissistic personality, hysterical personality, dependent personality, and a dissociative disorder not otherwise specified with respect to Danny's contention of being controlled at times by the demonic spirit Gemini. McMahon equated Danny's emotional and psychological developmental stage to that of a child.

As part of her process of diagnosis, Dr. McMahon had interviewed Rolling's brother, Kevin, on September 9, 1993. She found Kevin's memories of growing up to be considerably different from Danny's or other members of the family, but he also acknowledged having "great gaps" in his memory. Kevin did not dispute that instances of abuse happened; he just could not specifically recall most of them. However, he did acknowledge that he and Danny did not have a pleasant home environment.

"His statement was that growing up in that household was not good," McMahon recalled. "It was not a good place to be; and he could not wait to get away from there [because] it was a very strict place."

When discussing his brother, Kevin described how Danny could be both "cruel and gentle." Danny had set fire to a turtle when he was 13, but he could also be "gentle enough that a butterfly will land on his finger and he will hold it." Kevin said that he was "shocked" when he heard about the homicide allegations against his brother. "The Danny I knew and grew up with couldn't have done this," he insisted. "He couldn't stalk somebody down and murder them, not unless he's flipped. I cannot imagine it."

Kevin also told McMahon about an event that traumatized Danny when he was about 12 years old. His father came home from work one day and kicked the family dog so severely that the dog died a couple of days later. As Kevin recalled, "Danny was furious at the dog for dying, picked it up and flung it across the yard. He just couldn't cope with it."

Asked to explain how Danny ended up as a rapist and murderer while Kevin led a law-abiding life when they had grown up in the same environment, Dr. McMahon reframed the question.

> They are not raised in the same environment. It is different, by virtue of the fact that you have two different children. They are treated differently by the parents. They react differently to the parents. And they take away, from any event, different things.

> All the way along [the history] talks about, from day one, the difference in how Danny reacted to this father, for instance, and how Kevin reacted to this father.
>
> They are two different individuals. They have reacted to what went on in the household very differently, and they now are two very different adults.

McMahon also discussed her interview of Agnes Mitchell, who lived near the Rolling family nearly all of Danny's childhood and who adamantly asserted that Danny had been abused by his father. She described James Rolling as "crazy, sick, barbaric, paranoid, abusive, a schizo, a killer, cruel to animals."

Mitchell recalled one event when Danny was 13 or 14 years old and his father did not like the way he had mowed the yard. She walked into the house and found James sitting with his knee on Danny's chest, pressing all of his weight down onto the boy. Danny was struggling to breathe, his face turning purple, as he pleaded with his father to stop. All the while, his father "was just laughing a crazy kind of laugh." Mitchell also remembered seeing Danny handcuffed by his father on at least three occasions, including one time with his hands bound behind him as his father whipped him with a rope. She tried to help, but anytime someone reported the abuse, the Shreveport Police Department would protect Rolling's father since he had been a cop there for so long.

Dr. McMahon explained that many of Danny's family members and friends viewed him as someone who "couldn't hurt a flea". According to McMahon, a borderline personality like Rolling typically acted at the two extremes, and most people saw only the side of Danny that he sees as himself:

"very gentle, loving, caring." She characterized him as "somebody, who for 98 or 99% of his lifetime has been on this good side. When we look at 98% of Danny's life, he's a mild-mannered guy. The other two percent is a whole different ball game."

When she asked Danny about his encounter with Gemini while serving time in Parchment Prison, he described Gemini as a "demon, an evil spirit" who found a "crack in his soul." While sitting in his cell, Danny decided that he would "become the world's greatest rapist, vent my frustration on the world. I could sense another presence. 'I can give you that revenge if you let me in.' So I did let him in."

~~~~~

Psychologist Sidney Merin agreed with Dr. McMahon's prior finding that Rolling did not have any impairment of brain function or anything suggestive of brain damage. McMahon estimated Rolling's IQ to be in the range of 110 to 115 in the "bright average" range.

~~~~~

The day before Valentine's Day, an article appeared in *The Washington Post* under the title: "Roses are Red. Blood Red." The featured article focused on the relationship between 46-year-old Sondra London and Danny Rolling. It opened with a quote from London: "Like many women I've had a weakness for good-for-nothing men," and it included an excerpt of a letter Rolling wrote to the paper: *My relationship with Sondra runs as deep as the Amazon River . . . and just as wild! She is an extremely exciting woman! She is without a doubt my soulmate*. Although London insisted that she was not "one of those death row groupies," the article suggested that her story might better be called "Men Who Butcher Women and the Women Who Love Them."

Chapter 21

Jury Selection and Trial

"It was like cutting butter" (Danny Rolling)

Jury selection in Danny Rolling's quintuple murder trial began on the day after Valentine's Day, February 15, 1994, over three years since the five Gainesville killings. Nearly 240 journalists obtained credentials to cover the trial being held in courtroom 4A of the Alachua County Courthouse in Gainesville, the largest courtroom in the county. Rolling's defense team of four lawyers, led by Alachua County Public Defender Rick Parker, had spent months preparing to defend him against the largely circumstantial evidence case prosecutors had equally labored to prepare. But the State of Florida's case barely began before a stunning development brought the proceedings to an unexpected halt.

Standing before Judge Stan Morris around 9:30 a.m. that morning, Rolling informed the court that he wished to enter a plea of guilty for all five of the murder counts as well as all three of the sexual battery counts he faced.

"Your Honor, I've been running from first one thing and then another all my life," the stone-faced Rolling told the judge, "whether from problems at home, or with the law, or from myself. But there are some things that you just can't run from."

Some of the spectators sitting in the courtroom gallery gasped. Others sat in stunned silence.

"When he walked in and confessed, we were all beside ourselves," George Paules, father of victim Tracy Paules, said later.

Unbeknownst to nearly everyone in the courtroom, Rolling had signed a written guilty plea at 10:00 p.m. on February 10, and his attorney informed Judge Morris and Alachua County State Attorney Rod Smith about the plea later that night. They had all agreed to keep the plea quiet until the trial date so that the victims' families could all be present when it was announced. The plea came the day after the prosecution had prevailed at an evidentiary hearing in which the judge ruled that a "replica weapon," a Ka-Bar knife like the one used in the killings, could be introduced into evidence. The State had also been granted the ability to introduce partial skeletal remains of the victims into evidence to show the jury the damage caused by the knife. The prospect of having the jury see both blade and bone may have factored into Rolling's decision to plead guilty.

Now, Judge Morris dutifully accepted Rolling's plea and scheduled jury selection for the penalty phase of the trial to begin the next day. Like any judge juggling a crowded court calendar, Morris welcomed a plea that promised to free up his docket. After all, the guilt phase of Rolling's trial had been expected to last up to 10 weeks with nearly 150 witnesses. The surprise plea saved substantial expense and effort in a case that had already exceeded $5 million in investigative and pretrial costs.

Afterward, Rolling's attorney revealed that he had decided to plead guilty because he wanted to spare the families of his victims from having to hear the gruesome details of the murders.

"He thinks it is the right thing to do," Rick Parker explained.

"That's bullshit," exclaimed Tracy Paules's mother upon hearing Parker's explanation of his client's motivation. "He is a liar. He has no remorse for those five people. This was just a ploy. He is scared to death he is going to get the electric chair, and I hope he does."

Local Gainesville attorney Steven Glazer, who represented serial killer Aileen Wournos for her guilty plea in five murder cases, pointed out that Rolling's plea offered him two benefits. First, it cast him in a remorseful light in the eyes of the jury that would decide whether to impose the death penalty. Second, it decreased the jury's exposure to the shocking details of the murder scenes, which would certainly help his defense attorneys' efforts as they tried to portray him in a sympathetic light by emphasizing his abusive upbringing.

Tampa prosecutor Mike Benito offered another possibility: "You're dealing obviously with a very, very sick mind. Maybe he's so sick he's decided he wants people to know he did all this stuff. He may get some pleasure out of that."

Regardless of Rolling's true motivation for pleading guilty, lead prosecutor Rod Smith vowed to seek the death penalty against him.

"These crimes warrant the death penalty," Smith proclaimed. "We now know who was the slayer of the Gainesville students. He didn't get a deal. He pled because he did it. And with all due respect, we were going to prove that he did it."

Edward Humphrey, once the prime suspect in the case, expressed his relief about the confession.

"I'm just really happy that it looks like it's all over with," he said, "and it's a big relief for me and my family. I'm just hoping it's all over so I can get on with my life."

University of Florida President John Lombardi voiced the perspective of many in the Gainesville community.

"We are relieved that our legal system has answered with certainty the question of who committed the crimes," Lombardi said. "On the one hand, we're delighted there is clear closure as to the question of guilt. But on the other, nobody will have closure to the pain, to the loss, the scar it leaves on your soul."

On February 17, as jury selection proceeded in the penalty phase of Rolling's case, an editorial appeared in the *St. Petersburg Times* addressing possible reasons for Rolling's plea, while providing a reminder about Edward Humphrey's mistreatment during the investigation and trial process.

> *For a man whose life somehow went so terribly wrong, Rolling at least did the right thing Tuesday when he made his courtroom confession. While some smell a legal strategy in Rolling's guilty plea, it seems more likely that Rolling was, for his own reasons, ready to tell his story.*
>
> . . . . .
>
> *If authorities act responsibly, Rolling's plea also should clear Edward Humphrey from the cloud that has hung over his young life since law enforcement officials first named him as the "prime suspect" shortly after the murders. Humphrey, who apparently was guilty only of being mentally unstable and in Gainesville at the time of the murders, was another victim in this case.*
>
> *Humphrey was victimized by investigators and prosecutors who leaked his name to reporters without taking public*

responsibility for having done so. He also was victimized by the media, which published stories based on those leaks without following the normal safeguards to prevent inaccurate and/or unattributed allegations from being aired.

While some of the early lapses of good judgment by investigators and the media were understandable given the pressures created by the horror of Rolling's crimes, Humphrey deserves much better than he received Tuesday from State Attorney Rod Smith. Smith stopped short of clearing Humphrey, saying only, "I'm not anticipating that he's going to be charged."

If Smith has some evidence of Humphrey's complicity in this case, it is past time for him to present it. If he doesn't, he should say so straightforwardly – and offer an apology to Humphrey and his family while he's at it.

~~~~~

Based on the responses provided by members of the jury pool, Rolling's attorneys became concerned that prejudicial attitudes towards him would prevent them from obtaining an impartial jury for his sentencing trial. On February 25, they filed a motion for change of venue, arguing that the sentencing proceedings needed to take
~~~~~

place somewhere other than Alachua County to ensure a fair trial. Dr. Raymond Buchanan, a professor of communications at Pepperdine University, assisted the defense team during the jury selection with publicity analysis, jury profiling, and juror selection. He considered the potential for juror prejudice to be extremely high if the case remained in Alachua County.

"I couldn't recall a case that had more pretrial publicity than the Rolling case. The sheer volume of the publicity was just staggering," Buchanan said. It even exceeded the publicity of Ted Bundy's trial, which Buchanan had also worked on. The magnitude of the jurors' bias hit him after Rolling's guilty plea.

"After that guilty plea, it was my observation that people in Gainesville were more than just stunned. The reactions were of anger and distaste . . . the fear which had generated the anger in that community really was an awesome power."

Assistant Public Defender Dave Davis, with 22 years of experience practicing criminal law including 80 capital cases, reached a similar conclusion about the jurors' states of mind. He emphasized how "extraordinarily traumatized" and "terrorized" the Gainesville community had been by the 1990 murders.

> This is the first case, and only case I've ever seen where the animosity – I mean, when I say "palpable," the words escape me to describe the impression I got, not only from voir dire, but from the newspaper articles, of just the fear, the terror, the hatred of Danny Rolling, from a traditionally liberal community.
>
> . . . . .

> It's like they've all gone to the beach and here comes Jaws swimming out in the water. It's that sort of terror that just freezes the community. And they were absolutely terrified about it.

After a brief hearing, Judge Morris denied Rolling's motion for a change of venue, ruling that the trial would remain in Gainesville. As the attorneys readied their cases, University of Miami law professor Steve Winter opined that the defense team's effectiveness in getting the jurors to understand why Rolling committed the five murders would be the most significant factor influencing whether they returned a verdict recommending that he be executed for his crimes.

"The real issue at the death penalty phase is the degree to which the jury sees him as a human or as a demon," Winter explained. "The difference between life and death is not the degree with which the jury excuses what he did, but the degree to which they understand why he did it."

On March 7, 1994, Rod Smith gave the prosecution's opening statement to the three-man, nine-woman jury panel. During his 80-minute summation detailing the grisly events of August 1990, Smith portrayed Rolling as a careful hunter who meticulously planned the five student murders. He began by describing how the "shrewd" and "methodical" Rolling acquired the knife used to end the lives of his five Gainesville victims.

> On July 18, 1990, Danny Harold Rolling walked into an Army-Navy store near the bus station in Tallahassee, Florida. He made a purchase. He spent about $34.00. The item purchased was a Marine Corps Ka-Bar knife. The State will prove to you that

> the reason he selected this particular knife is that Danny Rolling considered it the "best knife for killing." It would slash through flesh and bone. In a very real sense, that purchase began an episode that will forever be remembered as the Gainesville Student Murders.

Smith then recounted how, after finishing the taped message to his family, Rolling prepared for his killing spree. Dressed in the "clothes of a killer," wearing "dark colors for the dark night and a dark purpose," Rolling left his hidden campsite in the woods and crept toward an area of houses. He stole a bicycle behind one of them and made off on his new mode of transportation.

After he pedaled past a hospital, the night suddenly brightened with red lights. A police patrol car pulled up beside him.

"What happened to your light?" asked the uniformed cop behind the wheel.

"What light, officer?" Rolling replied.

"You have to have a light on your bike after dark."

Rolling's raised eyebrows expressed his surprise. He explained that he had just moved to town and was on his way to a party, but he had gotten lost. The officer must have heard similar stories before because he did not seem surprised. He smiled understandingly and gave Rolling directions, reminding him to get a light for his bike.

"I definitely will," Rolling assured him. "Thanks, officer!"

He pedaled away, amazed at his luck and eager to resume his nighttime hunt, "roaming the Southwest area of Gainesville preparing to commit rape and murder." He initially targeted a single woman for his first victim, after spotting her while peeping into her windows. The predator prepared to pounce on his unsuspecting prey, only to be thwarted at the last moment. Startled by two approaching students, Rolling fled the scene.

A short time later, he walked to another apartment complex. As he spied on two girls from the bushes outside their room, a security guard suddenly appeared and asked what he was doing. Although he avoided being caught, he was again forced to flee.

Around 3:00 a.m., Rolling ended up at the entrance to Wiliamsburg Village Apartments. After leaving his bike out front, he pulled a brown ski mask over his head and walked around to the back of the apartment building. He found his way to the deck of apartment 113 where he saw Sonja Larson and Christi Powell inside. This time no one disturbed him as he watched and waited, lurking just outside their window.

He tried to open the back door of the apartment, but it would not budge, so he wedged a screwdriver into the door frame near the lock. He gripped the door handle again and this time it turned. He stepped into the silent, unlit apartment. As he walked through the kitchen and into the living room, he saw Christi sleeping on the couch. He crept over and stood above her, watching the slow rhythm of her breathing. Then he continued on to the staircase and silently ascended to the upper floor. At the top of the stairs, he tiptoed across the hall and entered a bedroom. Inside, Sonja Larson lay sound asleep on her bed. He slowly stepped beside her. After readying his Ka-Bar knife and a piece of duct tape, he struck. As he pressed the tape over Sonja's mouth, he thrust the knife blade deep into her chest.

Cruelly jolted awake, Sonja cried out in pain, but barely made a sound because of the tape covering her lips. Eyes wide open and filled with terror, Sonja flailed around trying to defend herself, but she stood no chance against the flurry of piercing thrusts that followed. She soon succumbed to the cold, unforgiving steel and, after a few more seconds, she lay silent and still.

The first deed done, Rolling calmly walked back down the stairs and over to Christi, still sleeping peacefully. Covering her mouth with his hand, he cruelly woke her, brandishing the knife blade, and warning that she better stay quiet. Confused and afraid, Christi silently nodded her assent. Rolling pulled her down onto the carpet and raped her until he ejaculated. Then having satisfied himself, he pushed her onto her stomach and stabbed her in the back, over and over again until she stopped moving and faded away.

Done with Christi for the moment, he returned to Sonja upstairs. Pulling her to the edge of the bed, he took off her underwear and spread her legs, but the bloody condition of her body repelled him from raping her. Instead, he left her like that, careful to remove the strip of tape from her mouth before going back downstairs. After having his way with Christi's corpse, he found some dishwashing soap in the kitchen and cleaned out her vagina. Then he walked out of the apartment, retrieved his bike, and disappeared into the black refuge of the night.

The next night he returned to a location that he had targeted several days before: Christa Hoyt's house. His previous time there he had spied on her from the dark outside her sliding glass door, watching the naked young woman as she emerged from the shower and walked around inside. Now he had come back to pay her a more personal visit. He pushed down a weakened part of the chain link fence behind her backyard and crept up to her door. Peering inside, he could see that no one was home so he pried open the sliding door and stepped inside. He searched for a good spot to ambush Christa when she returned, and decided on an alcove by the front door. To give himself room to hide, he removed a bookcase from the spot and dragged it into the bedroom. Then he crouched in the unlit entryway next to a window and waited for her to return.

At about 10:15 p.m., he saw her walking up the sidewalk to the front door. He heard a jingling sound as she fumbled with her keys and then the click of the dead bolt as she unlocked the door. Christa stepped into the house, closing the door behind her and locking it back before placing her keys and racquetball gear on a nearby table. As she turned around, she hesitated for a moment as if suddenly aware of something not being right. But it was too late. Rolling sprang from the alcove and grabbed her tightly around the neck. He threw her to the ground and taped her hands behind her back before sticking duct tape over her mouth. And then he repeatedly raped her.

When he was at last done, he turned Christa over and stabbed her once in the back. She gasped silently in pain through the tape, her muffled cry no louder than a whimper. He watched excitedly until her heart stopped beating, then plunged the knife into her belly and sliced upward, eviscerating her with little effort and even less regret. Grabbing her breasts, he cut off each of her nipples and placed them on top of her protruding intestines. Later, he returned and cut off her head, using the razor-sharp knife like a scalpel to sever the head from its torso. Still not satisfied, he posed her body and propped her head on a bookshelf beside the bed, delighting in the gruesome scene of her head seeming to stare at its displaced body.

Of his five Gainesville victims, Christa lived the longest. It was about an hour from the time she came home until he killed her. It was an hour of brutal torture. It was an hour of unimaginable suffering. It was an hour of incomprehensible horror.

~~~~~

Rolling prowled the dark streets of Gainesville again on August 26, slinking through the shadows cast by the occasional street lights he passed. This was when he felt
~~~~~

most alive, anticipating the thrill of the kill. Feelings of inferiority and powerlessness vanished when he saw the fear in the eyes of his victims, knowing that they were helpless and completely under his control, their desperate horror reflecting his own despairing sense of self.

A little after 11:00 p.m., he wheeled his bike into the parking lot of Gatorwood Apartments. Leaning the bike on its side at the back of the complex, he slithered between several buildings until he came to a corner apartment. Sneaking closer, he peered in a lighted window and saw Tracy Paules laying on her bed. Wearing only a nightshirt, Tracy cradled a telephone against her ear. He watched in silence as she continued a conversation muted by the window.

Suddenly, he heard the sound of approaching footsteps. He instinctively ducked behind a bush as two young men came around the corner. Lost in their own conversation, they never noticed him lurking just a few feet away. They continued on past him and soon disappeared into the corridor of another building.

Emerging from his hiding place, Rolling resumed his dark vigil. He watched Tracy hang up the phone and climb into bed, pulling the covers up as if to ward off whatever evils might come calling in the night. Soon after Tracy went to bed, Manny Taboada steered his motorcycle into a nearby parking space and hurried inside. Rolling watched and waited. He lingered a while longer after all of the apartment's lights went out. Then the waiting was over.

At 3:00 a.m. he strode to the rear sliding glass door and used a screwdriver to carefully pop off the lock. Carrying a pistol and the same Ka-Bar knife used to kill his first three victims, Rolling stepped silently into the apartment. Treading softly down the hallway, he discovered Manny asleep in his bedroom. Rolling stood over him, paused to ready himself, then plunged the knife deep into Manny's chest, guiding the blade upward to pierce his heart.

Manny gasped violently awake.

"I've been shot!" he screamed in confusion and disbelief.

Rolling did not hesitate. He stabbed Manny in the abdomen again and again, slashing and cutting as Manny struggled to fend off the blows.

"Bastard!" Manny exclaimed through the pain, staring up at his attacker. As the sheets around him turned wet and red, he sighed and uttered with his last breath, "Tracy."

After watching Manny die, Rolling stepped out of the bedroom into the hallway. As soon as he did so, he saw Tracy standing at the entrance to her bedroom down the hall. She screamed and slammed the door closed behind her. Rolling charged after her like a predator chasing down its prey. He kicked the door open and stormed into the room knife in hand. Tracy stared at him in horror.

"You're *him*, aren't you" she gasped.

"No," he replied, his voice a low growl.

"Yes, you are," she muttered numbly, already resigned to her fate.

Pouncing on her, Rolling pushed Tracy onto her stomach, bound her wrists with duct tape, and then turned her back over.

"You're going to get caught," she suggested feebly, more a desperate final plea than a challenge.

"Maybe," he replied, his tone resolute and vengeful. "But not tonight."

Tearing off her nightshirt, he forced her legs apart, dropped his pants, and violently penetrated her. As he thrust into her, she pleaded for him to stop.

"Please," she begged, "it hurts."

Her plea fell on deaf ears.

"Take the pain, bitch!" Rolling bellowed before pounding her even harder.

When he finally spent himself, he turned Tracy onto her stomach again. Pressing her face roughly into her pillow, he thrust the razor-sharp knife into her back, stabbing her repeatedly until she lay still.

Throughout the prosecutor's grim narrative of the murders, family members and friends of the five slaughtered students huddled together in the back of the courtroom gallery for support, struggling to endure hearing the gruesome details of their children's deaths. Among them was Tampa resident, Joyce Burton. She knew exactly what they were going through and fully shared in their grief. Burton had lost her daughter, her only grandson, and her ex-husband when Rolling murdered them in Shreveport in 1989. Over the past months and especially during the trial itself, Burton had grown close to the Gainesville families.

"When I walked in that room for the first time and met them, it was like I had known them forever," she explained. "We each know how the other one feels. We each know that this person robbed us of the rest of our lives of joy."

Burton vowed to attend all of the trial and looked forward to being there to see Rolling's final sentence.

"I want to see his reaction when the judge reads the verdict and sentence," she said with a fierceness in her eyes.

~~~~~

After detailing all five killings to the jury, Smith discussed the aggravating factors that would support the imposition of the death penalty against Rolling, including that he had 12 prior convictions for violent crimes in four different states: Florida, Alabama, Georgia, and Mississippi. As he concluded, Smith confidently assured the jurors that the
~~~~~

evidence "will not only show you the cold, calculated manner in which Danny Rolling carried out his murderous plans, but also the heinous, atrocious, and cruel manner in which he snuffed out each of these young lives."

In his opening statement for the defense, Chief Assistant Public Defender Johnny Kearns emphasized Rolling's unstable, abusive home environment. He stressed to the jurors that Rolling should not be given the death penalty because he suffered from mental illnesses causing him to have such frequent "breaks with reality" that it earned him the nickname "Psycho" from fellow inmates.

~~~~~

At 5:30 p.m. on the same day as opening statements, psychologist Daniel Sprehe sat for deposition. Dr. Sprehe testified that during his examination of Rolling, he found him to be a "really bright person" and estimated his IQ to be in the "lower end of the bright average range . . . starting from 110." His principal diagnosis of Rolling focused on antisocial personality disorder, as opposed to borderline personality, largely because Rolling "was cool and in control and not acting in an angry manner" during his murder spree, which entailed "a lot of planning," such as procuring the equipment to commit the crimes and wearing gloves as part of "carrying out an intricate plan" to avoid detection. As further explanation for his diagnosis, Dr. Sprehe opined that borderline personalities "are always known to be really angry people," whereas Danny did not usually act that way.

Sprehe rejected the notion that Gemini or some demonic spirit took possession of Rolling and compelled him to commit his crimes. Instead, Sprehe believed that he made them up afterward in an attempt to distance himself from the brutality of what he had done.

> His use of Gemini or Ennad, these are largely post-facto sorts of thing . . . He needs to externalize it because his behavior is not
~~~~~

> consistent with what he would like to think of himself. But it has nothing to do with dissociation. It has nothing to do with demonic possession. It has nothing at all to do with any dissociative trance state. It has to do with the way he has of externalizing it so he can call it something.
>
> When we attach a name to something . . . we can use it in whatever way we want to, including trying to exculpate ourselves.

Rather than being caused by demonic possession, Rolling's crimes could be traced back to his childhood:

> A personality disorder develops insidiously over many, many, many years, all the way back to childhood, and it's reinforced until it becomes such a part of the individual's life, that they don't really see it as being alien to themselves, as they might with a phobia or a depression, or a compulsion, or something of that nature.

Dr. Sprehe pointed to Rolling's insistence that Bobby Lewis be the mouthpiece for his confession to the Gainesville slayings as an example of Rolling's need to be in control, the same need that served as a contributing motivation for the rapes and murders he committed. As Sprehe put it, the format of the confession constituted a "kind of game, but it was his game, and he played by his rules."

Back in Courtroom 4A, prosecutor Rod Smith showed jurors a Ka-Bar knife identical to the one Rolling had used to kill his five Gainesville victims. Smith repeatedly unsheathed the knife, stabbing at the air to recreate the savage attacks. To emphasize the effect and ensure a lasting imprint on the minds of the jurors, he displayed bloody pieces of the victims' clothing, including the blood-stained shirts of Sonja Larson and Manny Taboada.

Ka-bar Knife

~~~~~

As the jury continued evaluating evidence during Rolling's penalty proceeding, Edward Humphrey traveled to Tallahassee on March 9 seeking to have his civil rights restored that were lost due to his conviction for the battery of his grandmother. Now an honors student at Brevard Community College, Humphrey needed his rights restored
~~~~~

so that he could achieve his goal of becoming an X-ray technician.

"I never intentionally hurt anyone in my life," he said. "I was hurt very badly, and I believe I was given this harsh punishment mainly because at the time I was the prime suspect in the Gainesville murders. But I'm leaving that behind me. I want to get on with my life."

Due to his history of mental problems and a 1992 arrest for under-age drinking, the Florida Parole Commission recommended rejecting Humphrey's clemency request, and Governor Lawton Chiles made a motion to deny the request before realizing that Humphrey wished to personally address the clemency board.

Stepping before the board, Humphrey told the Governor and his Cabinet members that he deserved a fresh start. Following Humphrey's statement and comments by his attorney, Chiles and the rest of the board agreed to reconsider Humphrey's request. The Governor and at least three of the six Cabinet members would have to side with Humphrey for his request to be granted.

~~~~~

The next day back in Gainesville, jurors listened to a 58-minute tape recording that Rolling had made on August 4, 1990, in a Sarasota motel room and on August 23 at his Gainesville campsite, only hours before killing Sonja Larson and Christi Powell. As his recorded voice played through the courtroom loudspeakers, Rolling sunk in his chair, closing his eyes at times and covering his face with his hands.

The tape, recovered from Rolling's camp the day after the murders of Manny Taboada and Tracy Paules, began with Rolling addressing his mother, father, and brother.

"No matter what anybody thinks about this man, Danny Harold Rolling, I want these three people that I'm talking to right now to know that this is not the road I wanted.
~~~~~

This is not what I wanted, but it is the road that is before me now, and I will walk it like a man."

He gave individual messages to each of his family members, starting with his father.

> You know I love you, Pop, and I'm so sorry Dad. It rips my heart out by the roots to think what happened between you and I. I'm sorry, Pop. If it means anything, I'm so very sorry. And I suffer a lot behind this. I hurt in my heart. And it never goes away, Pop . . . Nothing's ever been easy for me. Well, I always wanted to make you proud of me, Dad, but somehow or another I always fell short.
>
> . . . . .
>
> Mom, you're a precious, precious soul. There ain't a woman on the face of this earth that can cook like you can, sugar. You hear me? You got to be the best cook in the whole wide world. And believe you me, I miss it. I love you, Mom . . . And Mom, don't blame yourself for anything in the past. None of it's your fault. I don't really believe it's anybody's fault. It's just the way things happen sometimes. Sometimes we want so much for things to be right, especially with the ones we love. But it doesn't always happen that way, does it, Mom?

. . . . .

> Kevin, I love you . . . the last time I saw you, you said that I enjoy this. You're wrong, Kevin. I hate this. I hate what's happened. I hate the way I have to live. I'd trade it all, I'd trade both my arms, if I could go back and do it all over . . . You are good, as good as men go. I know that we're all basically evil. But there is some good in you, Kevin . . . I love you brother more than even words can even justify. I wished it could have been different. I wanted so much for you and I to strike out together, and make a dent in this world, and make something out of our lives.

After delivering the three messages, Rolling spent a large portion of the tape singing eleven songs that he had written, with titles such as "Comin' Down on You," "Boggy Bayou," "I Need a Job," "Broken Hearts," and "Chaingang Living." Two songs seemed particularly relevant to his situation.

"Jesse James," he said, "kinda depicts the way that really my life is. I guess in a way Jesse James and myself, yeah, we're both having to live the same life, the life of an outlaw." In the lyrics, Rolling sang of a man "who chose a life of crime" and whose "robberies he planned with passion and joy". He hesitated about playing another song, "Mystery Rider," before finally deciding to sing it:

> Mystery rider . . . what's your name?

> You're a killer, a drifter gone insane.
>
> Mystery rider . . . what's your game?
>
> You're a rebel no one can tame.

The tape resumed several weeks later when he was in Gainesville. He recorded the second part at nightfall in his camp.

> I'm in a different place than the last time I recorded. Now I got the sky for a blanket, the earth for a bed, and some rumpled-up clothes for a pillow, but it's OK. It's just the way it is, you take the good with the bad . . . I just wanted you all to have something to remember me by. Listen to those crickets, man, well . . . I'm kinda lost for words. I really am. Just sittin' here thinkin' about what to say, and I really don't know what to say. . . I know I'll have to run the rest of my life. But I'm gettin' pretty good at it, if that means anything. Shoot, I've been stopped by the PO-lice I don't know how many times, checkin ID's and stuff. I guess I'll make do. I hope I do.

As the audiotape wound to a close, Rolling again addressed his father, before concluding on an ominous note:

> You know, Pop, I don't think you was ever really concerned about the way I felt anyway. Nope, I really don't.

> You never would take time to listen to me. Never cared about what I thought or felt. I never had a daddy that I could go to and confide in with my problems. You just pushed me away at a young age, Pop.
>
> I guess, you and I, we both missed out on a lot. I wanted to make you proud of me. I let you down. I'm sorry for that.
>
> Well, I'm gonna sign off for a little bit . . . I got something I gotta do.

The Gainesville Ripper began his bloody killing spree a few hours later.

After hearing the tape, jurors watched an hour-long video of Rolling confessing to the crimes by whispering to inmate Bobby Lewis in response to investigators' questions. During the video, Rolling expressed regret for what he had become.

"I never wanted to come this way, believe me," he told detectives. "God as my judge, I never wanted to come this way. But I'm here, and now I've got to live with this. I ain't got nobody to blame but myself. But I want to understand as much as anybody because it's all so bad."

He spoke about different personalities or parts of himself that took over at various times, and remarked that he wished he could be a better person, all the while insisting that he felt bad about what he had done.

"People say Danny has no remorse. They don't know Danny. I don't know how I live with myself. I'm not proud of myself and my life."

Investigator Legran Hewitt asked him, “If you had something to say to these victims’ families, Danny, what would it be?”

Rolling paused in thought before answering.

“I would say to them that I don’t ask them to have pity on me. But I would ask them if they could find it in their heart to forgive so that the bitterness and the hatred about all of this won’t destroy what is left of their lives. I believe somehow through all of this that the Lord will give them strength. I can’t do anything for them. If I could, I would. I can’t.”

He looked across the table at Hewitt.

“What can I do for them?” he asked. “Tell me.”

“I have no idea,” Hewitt replied. “I think you’re doing the best you can and that’s telling them what happened there that night to their children.”

As Hewitt’s words sank in, Rolling leaned over, hid his face in his hands, and began to weep.

“Oh, God,” he sobbed.

~~~~~

On March 11, inmate Russell Binstead testified that in planning the murders, Rolling “wanted to invoke terror” and “wanted to leave everybody something to think about.” He produced a poem, titled “Gemini,” that Rolling had written and given to him. Parts of the ominous poem seemed to evoke the very methods that Rolling later used during his murderous Gainesville rampage:

Your nightmare come to life . . .

A maniac with a knife

The moan . . . the groan
~~~~~

The silver moon shown [sic]

The whisper . . . the cry

Dead leaves fly

Tonight . . . in the arms of Gemini

A captured butterfly will die

. . . . .

The whisper . . . the cry

Into the night comes Gemini

And tonight . . . you die.

Rolling had shared with Binstead how he struggled to keep the impulse to kill at bay, bottled up in the depths of his soul. He claimed that he could maintain control during the day, but Gemini took over at night.

It was Gemini that drove him to kill, and Binstead described Rolling's account of the horrific efficiency of his Ka-bar knife both during and after the killings.

"It went in like butter and came out like butter," Rolling told him.

Binstead also recounted how Rolling told him that he wished he had raped Sonja Larson instead of Christi Powell because she "was a lot prettier and had a better body". Binstead had been surprised to hear that Rolling made Christi perform oral sex on him before raping her.

"That was kind of stupid," Binstead had said to him. "What if she bit your dick off?"

In reply, Rolling had flashed an amused grin.

"She was too scared," he said. "Terrified. She would have done anything at that point. She thought if she pleased me she'd live."

~~~~~

On March 14, the prosecution rested its case. For the defense, Rolling's attorneys presented the three-hour videotaped testimony of Claudia Rolling, who could not travel to the sentencing hearing in Gainesville due to complications from liver cancer. Recorded in 1992, Claudia Rolling's testimony described her husband's terrible temper and aggressive acts against the family. She said that James Rolling verbally abused Danny every day, sometimes beat him, and never showed him any affection. The unyielding abuse by his father eventually changed Danny.

"He was always trying to get rid of that – that person that his daddy made him believe that he was," Claudia said. "He had no self-esteem. No self-worth."

She also testified that when James was a boy he had seen his own grandfather slit his grandmother's throat from ear to ear at the kitchen table. His grandmother was soaking her feet in a pan of water when she was killed, and the image of the water turning red with blood was forever etched in James's memory. James's family also had a history of mental illness. One day, his uncle had watched his wife go to the store, then he laid down on the couch, put the barrel of a shotgun in his mouth, and pulled the trigger. Additionally, James's mother had severe mood swings and suffered from schizophrenia, while other family members had stints in mental hospitals.

Claudia also described an incident at the dinner table with Danny in 1988. He told her that he was "another person" and his voice changed to a "deeper, harsh" tone. "His face got real hard, almost no emotion there at all, just kind of a deadpan expression. If I didn't know him so well," she said, "I probably wouldn't have known it was him."
~~~~~

~~~~~

Testifying at trial on March 15, Dr. Harry Krop recounted his appointment by the court to serve as a psychological expert to evaluate Rolling in the Gainesville murder cases. His evaluations of Rolling for the murder cases commenced in February 1993 and involved over 22 hours of interviews. During direct examination, Assistant Public Defender John Kearns asked Krop whether Rolling had ever discussed his childhood with him.

"Can you just give me a synopsis of how he described his childhood?" Kearns asked.

Dr. Krop replied without hesitation.

"Probably the quote that I have from Danny that sums up what Danny described to me, in terms of his perception of his childhood, was that at night, he would pray to God that God would come and take his father away from him. He described a history of emotional and physical abuse by his father."

Rolling had expressed that his childhood had been "like living on the edge of a volcano." But he did not simply despise his father. The relationship was more complicated than that.

"He essentially described his anger," Krop testified, "and yet at the same time, love for his father . . . On the one hand, he would talk about abuse and being victimized by his father. On the other hand, he would talk about how he still to this day wishes that he could gain his father's love and respect and affection."

Krop also testified that Rolling had felt betrayed by his mother because she kept going back to his father even though he kept abusing her, often as Rolling watched or tried to prevent it, while also continuing the abuse of Rolling and his brother.
~~~~~

"I asked him about the worst abuse that he could remember," Krop stated.

> And it's interesting, because he described two different things; one physical, and one, what I would consider emotional.
>
> The physical was being beaten by a belt until he was black and blue and being hit in the face.
>
> And the other incident that he described to me was his father shaving his head the first day of school; which was not a physical abusive incident, but to him, was extremely humiliating, and he was ashamed at that time.

Krop also spoke about Rolling's past psychological assessments, including one by the Louisiana Department of Health in Shreveport in November 1988. Following that evaluation, the therapist had noted that Rolling "resented coming to the [hospital] to have one 'pick my brain,'" and that his "behavior was inappropriately hostile and sarcastic." He "denied all problems and took a demeaning view of psychiatry and those who worked in the field."

Dr. Krop reaffirmed his diagnosis of Rolling as having borderline personality disorder and antisocial personality disorder, adding sexual disorder paraphilia as another primary diagnosis due to Rolling's intense sexual urges and fantasies which he had acted upon by committing the rapes. During cross-examination by prosecutors, Krop acknowledged that Rolling had declared that he wanted other people to suffer like he had suffered and that the murders he committed had been fueled by a desire for revenge for the "things that had gone wrong" in his life.

“He was tired of feeling like his whole life had been nothing but suffering,” Krop confirmed. “He needed someone else to suffer.”

Rolling had also shared his belief that the worst way of dying would be “death in the night with a knife” because of how “horrifying” it would be to “know that you were going to die.” He enjoyed “holding the entire city hostage to fear” during the August 1990 murder spree, and admitted that he had peeked in Christa Hoyt’s window a few nights before her murder.

“He had watched her come out of the shower,” Krop confirmed. “He thought she was very attractive” and “he was stricken by how much she looked like his former wife”.

At the end of his cross-examination, Smith prompted Krop to admit that Rolling recognized that “we all have a choice of doing what’s right and doing what’s wrong” and whether to do “good or evil.”

“So when Danny Rolling chose to go in those apartments, he knew what he was doing, and every time he killed them, he made a choice to kill them, didn’t he?” Smith asked.

“Yes, he did,” Krop replied.

“And every time he stood over any one of them with a knife, he knew the difference between right and wrong, and he chose to do wrong, didn’t he, every time?”

“Yes.”

Smith let the deliberateness of Rolling’s actions leave a lasting impression on the jury.

~~~~~

On March 17, after the jury had been excused for the day, prosecutors complained to the judge that Rolling and juror Holly Sajczuk, a 23-year-old deli worker, had been inappropriately “smiling and nodding back and forth at each
~~~~~

other" at various times during the trial. Judge Morris acknowledged the acts, which were so noticeable that another juror had already written him a note complaining about Sajczuk's conduct, but he declined to speak to the jury about it since they were already near the end of the trial.

The next day, Rolling's ex-wife, Omatha Lummus, testified on behalf of the prosecution during its rebuttal case. As Omatha walked to the witness stand, Rolling watched her with hurting, hateful eyes. The petite brunette did not return his stare, making eye contact only once, and only for a moment, when Smith asked her to identify her ex-husband in court. Wearing a conservative, flowered dress, Omatha spoke with a soft Louisiana accent, answering Smith's questions matter-of-factly, her testimony meant to rebut the defense's evidence establishing James Rolling's years of physical and emotional abuse against his son.

Contrary to the defense's portrayal of James, Omatha testified that she never saw Danny argue with his father, that they "acted normal" together, and that Danny never told her about any abuse at the hands of his father. Instead, Omatha said that James had helped them out on many occasions, including by providing the newlyweds furniture, clothes, and groceries, and by helping Danny buy a car.

"We all got along just fine," Omatha asserted.

Smith wanted to emphasize the "normalcy" of the father-son relationship that she perceived.

"Did you ever see anything from his dad that indicated that he didn't love him?" Smith asked.

"No, I didn't," she answered plainly.

On cross-examination by Rolling's attorneys, Omatha conceded that she visited the Rolling family home infrequently, only once every week or two, and that the family did not talk to her about James and Claudia's numerous separations or Claudia Rolling's nervous breakdown.

"There may have been some things that I blocked out of this whole situation," she admitted, while also acknowledging that she "never questioned" her former husband about his feelings or any problems he might have had with his parents.

Afterward, Smith praised the effectiveness of Omatha's testimony, particularly with respect to her interactions and impressions of Rolling's father.

"I loved her testimony," Smith asserted. "I find it very credible. The James Harold Rolling she recalled certainly didn't appear to be a monster."

Omatha's appearance in court visibly rattled Rolling, upsetting him so much that he had to be calmed down afterward by his attorneys. The day after her testimony, the *Gainesville Sun* reported that Omatha *looks much like the young women Rolling raped, murdered and mutilated*. The newspaper story included the haunting observation that Omatha *bears a striking resemblance to Christa Hoyt*.

On March 20, Sondra London defended herself against accusations that she had formed a relationship with Rolling solely for financial gain. Rather than seeking to profit, she had repeatedly refused to sell Rolling's songs or market his art work.

"I'm not glamorizing Danny Rolling," she told the *Florida Times Union*. "I'm not taking the convenient position where the criminal is the villain . . . People do want to understand what goes on in the mind of the offender and no one else has the nerve and the courage to do what I'm doing."

~~~~~

Prosecutors completed their rebuttal case on March 21 with testimony from psychologist Sidney Merin. Dr. Merin acknowledged that Rolling had grown up in a hostile home environment, but he rejected the notion that Rolling had
~~~~~

been under distress at the time he committed the Gainesville murders.

"He was experiencing no more stress at the time of these events here in Gainesville as he was a month before, six months before, a year before, 10 years before," Merin stated.

He said Rolling lacked a strong conscience or healthy sense of empathy.

"He has what I would refer to as a Swiss cheese sort of conscience," Merin explained. "Sometimes it holds and he drives children to church, but most of the time, it just goes right through those holes."

Dr. Merin also disputed testimony from Rolling's medical experts that he suffered from borderline personality disorder, antisocial personality disorder, and paraphilia, and that he was mentally ill at the time of the student slayings.

"To characterize what he has done, what he has admitted to, as a borderline personality disorder . . . is to suggest that what he had done would be a schoolboy prank, rather than as a function of the violent behavior that would be associated with sadistic psychopathy."

The prosecution and defense presented their closing arguments on March 23. Family members of the victims, media personnel, and members of the Gainesville community crowded into the courtroom, anxious to witness the conclusion of the case that had plagued them for so many months. The courtroom gallery buzzed with anticipation as Rolling, surrounded by six deputies, shuffled to the defense table. Wearing reading glasses, a blue blazer, and dark tie, Rolling looked all around the courtroom, seemingly pleased to have a packed house as his audience.

State Attorney Rod Smith presented his closing argument first. Shortly before 10:00 a.m., Smith stepped solemnly to the podium. He reminded the jury that Rolling knew exactly what he was doing when he murdered Sonja

Larson, Christi Powell, Christa Hoyt, Manny Taboada, and Tracy Paules.

The killings had been planned well in advance by a "chameleon-like character," a "predator who stalked out the ground on which he was going to prey." Rolling had set out to commit them purposefully, the sheer brutality of the killings intended to secure his place as the "superstar of crime."

"Now he's committed five murders," Smith continued, "and I guarantee you nobody committed worse murders than these. These are legendary murders. These aren't just murders you hear about or read about. These are murders you never forget about. If these crimes do not justify the death penalty, it defies imagination what kinds of crimes would have to exist to justify such a recommendation."

He held up a large photograph of each victim's body at the crime scenes as he described them one by one. Black tape covered parts of the photos deemed so gruesome that they might otherwise prejudice the jury against the defense.

"That is what he left," Smith said, showing a photo of Sonja Larson's nude and bloodied body posed on her bed with her legs spread wide apart.

"This was Christina Powell when Danny was through," he said, brandishing another photograph.

"This was Christa Hoyt as Danny Rolling left her," Smith said, showing a picture of her decapitated and mutilated corpse propped upright on the edge of her bed.

Manny Taboada had fought ferociously against his attacker to no avail.

"Thirty-one stab wounds and you lose," Smith stated, while holding up a photo of Taboada's bloodied body.

Tracy Paules's death may have been the most terrifying of them all since she knew that a killer was on the loose when Rolling struck.

"She knew that there was only one way this would end," Smith said sadly, "and that was when he killed her."

He held up one more picture, this one of Tracy's body following Rolling's assaults, having raped her both before and after death. "That's the end for Tracy Paules," Smith somberly pronounced.

The gruesomeness of the photographs seemed to affect even Rolling. At one point during Smith's presentation, Rolling leaned over to his attorneys.

"I've got to get out of here," he whispered, his face tired and pale.

When Smith finished showing the photos, he came to the end of his argument.

"If you shirk away from today's duty, you will never forgive yourselves," Smith warned the jury as he concluded. For Rolling's "heinous, atrocious and cruel" crimes, Smith argued, "prison is simply not enough."

Closing argument from the defense attorneys came next. Deputy Public Defender Johnny Kearns pleaded with the jury to properly take into consideration the abusive upbringing Rolling experienced and how such an unhealthy environment during his formative years had caused permanent damage to his emotional and psychological health.

"If you looked at the crime scene photos, you don't need me to tell you that," Kearns said, before suggesting that life imprisonment would be the appropriate punishment for such a mentally disturbed individual.

"It's punishment because life is a sentence to Mr. Rolling of life without hope. It is the absence of hope which equals despair that is the punishment. No hope. Mr. Rolling is going to die in a small room, behind a brick wall covered with concertina wire, with a life sentence."

During his rebuttal argument, Rod Smith acknowledged that Rolling endured an abusive childhood and home environment, but he soundly rejected the suggestion that Rolling's unfortunate background excused his actions.

"Even if it was a bad house, so what? It wasn't as bad as how he left these homes," Smith proclaimed, pointing to the crime scene photographs. "You want to know what's a bad house?" he said, his voice rising. "It's a house after Danny Rolling visited it."

Then he pulled out the poem, "Gemini," that Rolling had written prior to the five murders. He read verses from the poem that paralleled what happened at some of the crime scenes. When he finished, Smith looked into the eyes of each of the jurors.

"When you return your verdict, that's when the nightmare will finally end," he assured them.

Now, after hearing eleven days of testimony, the jury would decide Rolling's fate.

Following the attorneys' nearly four hours of closing arguments, the twelve jurors began their deliberations at 4:00 p.m., tasked with determining whether to recommend the death penalty for Rolling. Unable to reach agreement by 10:30 p.m., the jurors were sent to a hotel for the night. They resumed deliberating the next morning, and after five-and-a-half hours reached a unanimous verdict.

Just before the jurors left the jury room, the lights flickered on and off in courtroom 4a, eerily mirroring the lights in Florida State Prison when power was diverted to the electric chair just before an execution. Then the jurors walked into court and took their places in the jury box.

Surrounded by five deputies, Rolling bowed his head as the court clerk read the verdict form.

"The majority of jury, by a vote of 12 to 0, advise and recommend to the court that it impose the death penalty upon Danny Harold Rolling."

Rolling showed little emotion after the phrase was repeated five times, one for each of the five murders. Seated in the front row of the gallery, Sondra London blew him a kiss. He replied with a sullen nod, before being led out of the courtroom.

The families of Rolling's victims comforted each other before giving a prepared statement:

> This is a shallow victory. Nothing will bring back Sonja, Christi, Christa, Manny, and Tracy. A sentence of death simply means that we will not live in fear that this killer will kill again. We continue to be haunted with the fear that people will remember this killer, even glorify him for the slaughter of our children. To our precious children, we love you and we desperately miss you.

They also vowed to see the death penalty imposed against Rolling.

"I want the man to die," said Laurie Paules, "I really do. He's going to fear for his life now, just as the kids did."

"It shouldn't take nine years for him to get the chair," added Servando Careaga, one of Manny Taboada's friends. "Something has to change."

Later, members of the jury sought to express the emotional toll of their task.

“To be honest, we felt like we had a life in our hands,” said juror Brenda Diaz. “As horrific as what he did was, he’s still a life. The most difficult thing was sitting in the jury room, and saying the word ‘death’ and hearing it said over and over. We all cried. It was not a task that we took lightly.”

“The pictures were horrendous,” juror Daren Stubbs explained. “They were like a stone wall that fell on everybody.”

After their final vote in favor of the death penalty, juror John Green had led the jury members in a prayer.

“Thank you for giving us the power to do this,” he said.

Chapter 22

Sentencing & Its Aftermath

"GOD DAMN that man! What he did to you was WRONG! It was EVIL! And to put the mask of GOODNESS over that EVIL is what made you exactly as you are."

(Feb 1993 letter from Sondra London to Danny Rolling)

On March 29, 1994, Judge Stan Morris held a hearing allowing prosecutors to present statements from the victims' families urging him to impose the death penalty, while likewise allowing defense attorneys to present mitigating factors that might sway the judge to choose life imprisonment for Rolling instead. Rolling's lawyers played a videotape of seven friends and relatives – his mother, brother, two aunts, a cousin, and two neighbors -- all pleading on his behalf. His mother's pleas particularly evoked empathy.

"When I held this little baby in my arms, I had no idea, no thought that he would be anything except a doctor or a lawyer, a president, anything big and wonderful," Claudia Rolling said. "And at a very young age, I saw changes in my son that I ignored. Changes that ultimately brought about the horror that we've gone through in the last two or three years."

Wiping away tears, she attempted to deflect any blame for the crimes from her son to herself.

> I've heard for a long time that children are the products of their environment. And if this is the case – and I believe it is – then take me because I would be the responsible one. I'm that one that was with him, that raised

> him. I'm the one that failed him somewhere.
>
> I beg for his life and I cannot imagine that taking one life will bring others back. And I want my son to live. I don't see him as the other people see him. I see him as the child I raised, a loving, gentle, kind little boy that grew into a young man.
>
> And I know that there would be people that would say he deserves it. That could very well be true, but I'm a mother and I love him. And I don't want him to hurt anymore because he's hurt all of his life.

Claudia Rolling's emotional appeal elicited sympathy from Christa Hoyt's stepmother, Diana, but did not diminish her desire for justice.

"She moved my heart," Hoyt said. "I feel sorry for her. He's her baby. But he's an adult now, and he's got to pay for what he did as an adult."

State Attorney Rod Smith read a letter from Sonja Larson's sister, Beth Devitt, describing how every holiday had been overshadowed by Sonja's death.

In November of 1990, I gave birth to my second daughter, Holly Jane, Devitt wrote. *Mom and Dad came to the hospital. I remember Dad sat for better than an hour holding Holly. We were supposed to be happy. But we cried. We worried. Knowing how deeply you are going to love this child, you ask yourself how can I bring her into this world of rage and hate and murder.*

Christi Powell's sister, Barbara Melcolm, wrote about the effects of Christa's murder on Melcolm's children, including her son Michael, who was 7 at the time.

The day before Christi left for school, she took Michael for a special day out. Later she called to say goodbye and tell him that it would be a long time before they could go on a date again. She said that she loved him and called him her handsome little ball player. Now Michael wears No. 17 on his uniform for the age he last saw Christi.

And Manny Taboada's old roommate, Sevando Careaga, described the guilt he felt about Manny's death.

I deeply regretted moving out of Gainesville and leaving Manny alone. We always took care of each other. However, I hadn't been there for him when he needed me the most. It was very hard to deal with the fact that if I would have remained his roommate, Manny would be alive today. But as long as I live, Manny's memory will never die. Nobody will ever be able to kill that.

Shuffling to the podium in leg shackles, Rolling addressed the judge last.

> There is much I'd like to say, Your Honor, about our world, my beliefs, and the destiny of man. However, I feel whatever I might have to say at this moment is overshadowed by the suffering I've caused. I regret with all my heart what my hand has done, for I have taken what I cannot return. If only I could bend back the hands on that ageless clock and change the past. But alas, I am not the keeper of time, only a small part of history and the legacy of mankind's fall from grace. I'm sorry, Your Honor.

Rolling's dramatic, two-minute apology did nothing to relieve the suffering of the victims' families, or their desire to see him put to death.

"I heard the words," said Sonja Larson's mother, Ada, "but the actions spoke loud enough."

Christa Hoyt's stepmother, Diana, had a similar reaction.

"I think he felt sorry he was caught, not that he did it," she said. "And if he was out right now, I think he'd do it again."

On the same day that Judge Morris listened to emotional appeals from the prosecution and defense in Gainesville, Shreveport authorities formally charged Rolling with the 1989 murders of Tom, Julie, and Sean Grissom.

"We are confident that Danny Harold Rolling is the person behind the three homicides," Police Chief Steve Prator announced.

Doug Burton, Julie Grissom's stepfather, expressed the family's relief that Rolling had finally been charged.

"We're glad now that this can come out and we can get on with our lives," Burton said. He did not feel cheated by the fact that Rolling would not face extradition for trial in Louisiana. To the contrary, forgoing that trial would spare the family from having to hear the horrifying details of the crimes in court.

Expressing his confidence that Rolling would, in fact, be sentenced to death in Florida, Caddo Parish District Attorney Paul Carmouche explained that the Louisiana warrant would not be pursued because doing so might enable Rolling to delay the Florida proceedings.

~~~~~

On April 18, almost four years after Edward Humphrey's conviction for the felony crime of assaulting his
~~~~~

grandmother, Governor Chiles signed an executive clemency order restoring his civil rights. Although happy to have his right to vote restored as well as the ability to obtain professional licenses in Florida, Humphrey stopped short of declaring that he had been given his entire life back.

"I don't think it will ever be an end for me personally," he said, "because I'll always have to live with these memories for the rest of my life."

~~~~~

Rolling's day of reckoning came on April 20, 1994. At 9:30 a.m. that morning, nearly thirty friends and relatives of his victims filed into the courtroom and took their place in the gallery, filling up the front three rows. Shortly afterward, deputies led Rolling, clad in a white shirt and tie, to the defense table. Then Judge Morris entered and made his way to the judge's bench. He wasted no time in getting the proceeding underway.

Reading from a prepared order, Morris recited the aggravating factors applicable to Rolling's sentence, including his extensive record of prior offenses, the calculated, premeditated nature of the five murders, his violent method of raping his victims before killing them, and the savage nature of the slayings. The judge spent considerable time emphasizing the "heinous, atrocious, and cruel" nature of the murders and how much each of the five victims suffered. The mitigating factors included the "small degree" of remorse that Rolling showed for his actions, the abusive home environment that Rolling experienced as a child, and Rolling's mental disorders. The judge found that, taken as a whole, the aggravating factors far outweighed those of mitigation.

The courtroom fell silent as he prepared to impose sentence.

"Danny Harold Rolling is hereby sentenced to death," he pronounced.
~~~~~

“Yes!” exclaimed Ricky Paules, unable to contain her emotion.

Judge Morris stopped reading the order and glanced over at her.

“I do not want any more outbursts,” he warned, before proceeding to announce four more death sentences. “Defendant committed for execution,” the judge concluded. “May God have mercy on his soul.”

Rolling revealed little emotion during the sentencing, other than nodding his head slightly and staring down at the table as the judge read the death sentences aloud. When deputies led Rolling out of the courtroom, Manny Taboada’s brother, Mario, stood up from his second-row seat in the gallery.

“Five years!” he bellowed at Rolling. “You’re going down in five. You understand that? In less than five years!”

After Judge Morris ordered his bailiff to escort the enraged man from the courtroom, Taboada turned to glare at Sondra London.

“And you! I’ve got something for you!” he snarled before being dragged away by the bailiff.

As Taboada reached the door, Sonja Larson’s brother hurried over to where Sondra London sat.

“From this moment on, you make one red cent from my sister, and we’re both coming after you,” Jim Larson warned. “We’ll both go down. I have nothing to lose. I’ll kill you.”

Visibly shaken, London shifted nervously in her seat, turning her head from side to side searching for someone who might help her.

“Did you hear that?” she asked frantically. “He just threatened me!”

Later, London released a copyrighted statement from Rolling expressing his relief to have the sentencing process completed.

Once it was done, I felt as if a big hairy smelly ape jumped off my shoulders and I could be human again, Rolling's statement read. *God Bless Gainesville, and Lord help heal its people. Amen.*

Despite his temporary relief about having the sentencing behind him, Rolling faced a future without freedom, saddled by the knowledge of the ever-receding road before him. The sentencing hearing had taken less than thirty minutes, but now Rolling would live the remaining years of his life in a small sterile cell, burdened by the cold realization that, despite the delays offered by legal appeals, he would end up counting down the last days of his life until the hour of his execution.

~~~~~

On July 27, Judge Morris entered an order granting the State Attorney's motion requesting non-disclosure of all photographs and videotapes depicting the five Gainesville victims at the crime scenes and Medical Examiner's Office. Supported by twelve affidavits from the parents and siblings of each of the victims, the motion asserted that "they wish to be harmed no further by being confronted in the media with the images of their slain and mutilated loved ones." In granting the motion, the judge noted that "common sense and experience dictated that no reasonable person could expect these claimants to face these images in a public forum without great emotional distress and trauma." To protect the victims' families while also upholding the media and public's right to access, the judge's order allowed members of the public to individually view the photographs and videotapes upon request to the clerk of the court.

After the formal imposition of Rolling's death sentence, five light-blue binders containing graphic 8-by-10-inch photographs of the crime scenes were made available
~~~~~

for viewing by appointment in 15-minute time slots in Room 110 of the Alachua County Courthouse. During the first few days of their availability, a line stretched down the block to view the photos. Secured in the clerk of court's office, the binders could only be viewed with a deputy sheriff and a clerk present in the room to monitor viewings and ensure no one took photographs of the binders' contents.

The families appreciated the precautions put in place.

"We did not want our loved ones to be put out there in the scenes where they were found, because he was a butcher, and he was cruel," Ada Larson explained.

Page one of the first binder started with the site of the first murders, the Williamsburg Village colonial style apartment of Christina Powell and Sonja Larson. The first photograph, encased in a clear plastic sleeve, showed the rear steps leading to the backdoor of the apartment. The next pictures showed the open back door and the girls' refrigerator stocked with orange juice, Ben & Jerry's Chunky Monkey ice cream, and the apples and bananas that Rolling ate after committing two grisly murders. Another showed a white-colored water ski hanging above Manny Taboada's bed, splattered red with blood.

Then came the photos of the bodies. Sonja lying in a pool of blood on her mattress. Christi's black and bloodied hands, her arms caked in dried blood. The horrifying images of Christa Hoyt's headless body, so gruesome that much of the graphic content had been cropped out.

Even with the strict viewing rules, Ann Garren did not like the thought of strangers staring at her daughter's bloody, battered body.

"So, how were those photos?" she shouted at people outside the courthouse as they came from their viewing appointments.

Years later, after he retired from the bench, Judge Morris insisted that he believed his ruling achieved a reasonable compromise of the competing interests involved.

"I was firmly convinced that the public has a right to know," he said. "I was trying to figure out a way to allow that access and to protect the families' sensitivities. I think I did that."

~~~~~

In August 1995, *Money* magazine rated Gainesville the best city in the country to live in, calling it a "leafy college town" with "sizzling" home values and "dazzling" job opportunities. In choosing Gainesville, *Money* explained that the city "offers a gracious charm and relaxed life that few U.S. spots can match." Ironically, the city's low crime rate contributed to its ranking at the top of the list.

Working as a night shift nurse at Shands Hospital, Diana Hoyt could not believe her eyes when she read the magazine's evaluation. She would never be able to associate the area with such positivity. It would forever be tainted in her mind as the "place where Danny Rolling used to hunt people to kill."

That same month, Ada Larson drove from her home in Pompano Beach to Mayfield Heights, Ohio, to visit her daughter's grave at Knollwood Cemetery. Larson made the more than 1,000-mile trip alone, a cassette tape of her slain daughter's voice serving as her only companion. She played the tape over and over again, navigating the loss and pain as she listened to Sonja singing Cindi Lauper's "Time After Time" and Amy Grant's "Love Will Find a Way." The families of Christi Powell, Christa Hoyt, Manny Taboada, and Tracy Paules did not have to travel as far to visit their children's graves at Arlington Park Cemetery in Jacksonville, Laurel Hill Cemetery in Archer, Vista Memorial Gardens in Miami Lakes, and Woodlawn Park North Cemetery in Miami, respectively. But their journeys were all just as difficult.
~~~~~

~~~~~

While his victims' families struggled adjusting to life without their loved ones, Rolling had long-since adapted to life on Death Row. Each day began at 5:00 a.m. with breakfast inside his bland, beige-colored, 6 by 9-foot solitary cell. Once a week, he was allowed to spend four hours with other Death Row inmates in the exercise area. But he spent most of his time reading, his usual materials consisting of the *Gainesville Sun* newspaper, *Popular Mechanics* magazine, and *Hustler*.

~~~~~

In late November 1995, State Attorney Rod Smith and Florida Attorney General Bob Butterworth met with the victims' families in Butterworth's Tallahassee office to hear their concerns about the glacial pace of Rolling's legal challenges to his death sentence. Frustrated by four extensions granted to Rolling's appellate attorneys by the Florida Supreme Court, the families vented their feelings for nearly two hours and voiced a united dedication to speed up the wheels of justice.

"It's very frustrating," said Jim Larson, Sonja's father. "It's been five years since our children died. The public needs to know that the judicial system doesn't seem to work for murder victims."

Mario Taboada echoed Larson's thoughts.

"I get more upset, the more I hear," Taboada said. "The system has failed us one more time."

Though there was little he could really do, Butterworth shared the families' outrage.

"This case is a prime example of how lawyers for capital defendants manipulate and abuse the court system for the sole purpose of delay," he asserted.

It would take nearly a year for Rolling's appeal to be heard by the Florida Supreme Court. Six years after his cold-blooded killing of five Gainesville students, Rolling's lawyers presented their arguments as to why his sentence should be reduced from the ultimate penalty of death to a "more humane" term of life imprisonment. The attorneys focused their case on the argument that the trial court acted improperly in refusing to change the venue of the sentencing proceeding to another part of the state. They insisted that, due to the extensive pretrial publicity of the case, it was impossible to seat an objective, impartial jury in Gainesville.

Ann Garren, mother of Christa Hoyt, watched the attorneys' oral arguments with exasperated disbelief.

"I want him to die," she explained with obvious agitation. "We don't get an appeal. Our sentence is done. Our children are gone."

~~~~~

Time passed as the families slowly started piecing their lives back together, never forgetting their beloved children and siblings, but determined to return to something close to normalcy. During the same time period, Rolling's case slowly slithered its way through the legal system. On March 20, 1997, the Florida Supreme Court finally reached its decision on Rolling's appeal. While recognizing that the three-week jury selection process had been "no small task" to complete, Florida's highest court deemed the trial court's "extensive" precautions sufficient to ensure that an impartial jury could be formed. In particular, the trial court had "allowed the parties wide latitude in questioning prospective jurors so that open animosity, as well as more subtle, unconscious prejudices, could be detected." This wide latitude, combined with the trial judge's liberal striking of jury pool members to whom the attorneys objected, enabled the parties to select jurors who were "without a doubt, impartial and unbiased." Based on its conclusion that the trial court's "intricate jury selection" ensured that an impartial jury had
~~~~~

been seated to hear the case, the Florida Supreme Court affirmed Judge Stan Morris's denial of Rolling's motion for a change of venue. Most importantly to the victims' five families, the court's ruling affirmed Rolling's five sentences of death.

~~~~~

Although Rolling had admitted killing the five Gainesville students, a jury had recommended that he be executed for his crimes, and a judge had sentenced him to death, the question of why he had chosen Gainesville for his heinous acts remained unanswered. Inmate and Rolling confidante Bobby Lewis suggested that Rolling's fascination with Ted Bundy played a part in the decision. He pointed out that when Rolling came to Florida, he first headed to Tallahassee where Bundy had killed two FSU students in 1978, and that Rolling had started his preparations to kill in that college town, even acquiring his murder weapon there, before deciding to go elsewhere. It seemed by happenstance that he ended up in Gainesville, which he "found to be a lot better area for his purpose."

~~~~~

As if the family of Sonja Larson had not suffered enough by losing her in the dead of night to a brutal killer, further tragedy came in broad daylight in the middle of the day on June 10, 1997. That morning, Carla Larson, the wife of Sonja's brother, Jim, went to her job as a construction engineer for a new resort near Disney World in Kissimmee, Florida. During her lunch break, she drove to a nearby Publix supermarket to buy some fruit. Shortly after 12:00 Noon on a sunny, summer day, a man walked up to her, punched her in the stomach, and abducted her.

John Huggins, a landscaper with a criminal record, had been staying at a motel across the street from the supermarket. He was on vacation with his wife and five kids. Like Danny Rolling, he struck without warning. After forcing Carla into her white Ford Explorer, Huggins drove to a remote field and strangled her to death. Her nude body was found in the field two days later, partially covered with sand and hidden in a thicket of palmetto plants.

Homicide detectives found their way to Huggins when his wife informed them that he had left her and the children in the motel at lunchtime on the day of the murder, and that when he returned later that afternoon, he was sweating and acting strangely. Investigators subsequently found Carla Larson's engagement ring hidden in Huggins's mother-in-law's house, stuffed in an electrical switch box.

When in 1990, seven years earlier, Jim Larson had heard the news of Sonja's murder, it had been Carla who wrapped her arms around him, reminding him of all of the good in life, promising that she would help him get through it and that she would always be there to support him. More recently, the couple had welcomed their first child, a daughter they named Jessica. Now Carla was gone, snatched away with the same gut-wrenching suddenness as Sonja.

~~~~~

Like Jim Larson, Sarasota resident Janet Frake was haunted by a terrible event from the past. Now she decided it was time to confront it, time to make peace with the past, time to tell the public what Danny Rolling did to her several years before on August 5, 1990, only a few weeks before his murderous rampage in Gainesville. After seeing news coverage of Rolling, she now knew the identity of her rapist.

"I have nothing to be ashamed of," she said, discussing why she decided to come forward. She hoped that talking about it might help other victims.

Then-30-year-old Janet had been home alone when evil came to her two-bedroom Clematis Street house unannounced that humid August night. Rolling, staying a short distance away at the Sunnyside Inn off Tamiami Trail, had spotted her while peeping in windows earlier that
~~~~~

evening. In a cruel twist of fate, he had watched the petite brunette as she lay in bed watching *America's Most Wanted*. He waited as she got up after the program ended, walked out the front door, and drove away. Then he broke into her house by removing several glass leaves from one of the bedroom windows. He waited inside until she returned two hours later from an outing to pick up beer and rent some movies.

Wearing a black ski mask and leather gloves, Rolling hid as she came in and then attacked her as she came out of the bathroom, binding her wrists and gagging her with duct tape. "Don't scream or I'll stab you!" he warned before leading her back into the bathroom and raping her. He told her that he was going to rape her all night long, then kill her and leave her body in the closet.

"At first I didn't think it was real," Janet remembered. "I thought somebody was playing a joke on me. But there was so much rage in him, so much anger."

A true crime and murder mystery aficionado, Janet had read that there was not one right way to react to a rapist. Sometimes fighting back enabled the would-be victim to escape, other times docile compliance ensured the victim's survival. Quickly assessing that she had no chance of resisting her significantly larger assailant, Janet decided to stay as calm as she could.

When Rolling told her that he planned "to do this all night," Janet mentioned that she had some cold beer in the fridge and asked if he wanted one. What happened next "was weird," but it saved her life.

"He went from one of the meanest, scariest, most violent sons of bitches you could ever imagine to being really calm and relaxed," she recalled.

After making her clean up in the shower, Rolling sat down at the table as she poured him a glass of Keystone Gold Beer. He asked her if he could take-off his ski mask, but she told him to leave it on. She secretly feared that if she saw his face, he would kill her.

Over their shared beers, Rolling told her about his difficult childhood and abusive father. In return, she recounted fictitious abuses about her own upbringing so that he would think she understood and could commiserate with what he had endured. The ruse worked. Rolling came to believe that his victim actually had feelings for him.

"You'd really like to date me if the circumstances were different," he said at one point.

They talked until 1:30 in the morning at which point she suggested that it was getting late and time for him to go. The now-docile Rolling agreed. Before leaving, he asked her to do him a favor and wait 10 minutes before calling the police. Then he walked out the front door.

Four years later, Janet saw him on TV pleading guilty to murder and she immediately recognized his voice. After getting over the shock of realizing that he was the one who had raped her, Janet recorded a videotape message to Rolling telling him the truth about what she thought of him. It was a therapeutic process, providing a much-needed venting of her anger. She later learned that Rolling refused to watch it.

Those in law enforcement believe that Janet would have died that August day if she had not been able to alter Rolling's state of mind. Whatever his reason for letting her live, Janet understood how lucky she had been.

"What I encountered that night was pure evil," she said. "That's what it was – pure evil."

And rather than torturing herself with the question of why Rolling had chosen her as his victim, Janet chose to focus only on the positive.

"Bad things happen to good people," she said, "but I think the good always survives."

Rolling had survived to rape again when, shortly after he left Janet's home, two Sarasota deputies stopped him as he walked across the street near the Sunnyside Inn. A female deputy asked for his I.D. and he handed her a Social Security card for "Michael Kennedy." The deputy told him that he matched the height and weight of someone who had reportedly been "scaring folks" in the area. When she asked what he was doing, Rolling explained that he had been at the hotel bar until last call and was walking to a nearby pancake restaurant for a late-night meal to help him sober up. Since a check of "Michael Kennedy's" identification came back with no warrants or violations, the deputy handed it back to him.

"You can go now," she said, and a killer was again free to walk the streets.

Chapter 23

Decisions & Explanations

"*I am not a monster*" (Danny Rolling)

On Friday, December 5, 1997, Sondra London stood outside the Alachua County Courthouse clutching a copy of *The Making of a Serial Killer*, a book she had co-authored with Danny Rolling. Wearing black high heels and a matching suit with a leopard-look collar, London stepped up onto a large block of grey stone. The words "Freedom of Speech" were chiseled into one side of the stone, "Freedom of the Press" was carved on the other. London intentionally chose this particular location, standing on the Speaker's Stone, a monument to the Bill of Rights, to produce a specific rhetorical effect.

"I stand on my constitutional right of free speech!" she proclaimed to the circle of television and newspaper reporters surrounding her.

London's defiant gesture reflected her legal posture in a lawsuit filed against her by the State of Florida under Florida Statute 944.512, popularly called Florida's Son of Sam law. The statute prohibited felons, or anyone acting on their behalf, from profiting from "any literary, cinematic, or other account of the crime for which [they] were convicted." The State's lawsuit sought all profits London made from selling *The Making of a Serial Killer* as well as $15,000 she was paid by *The Globe* tabloid for a five-part series of stories about the Gainesville murders.

Assistant Attorney General George Waas presented the State's case to the assigned trial judge during three hours of argument, contending that since London and Rolling were lovers and became engaged in 1993, they shared a "symbiotic relationship" which entitled the State to confiscate the proceeds sought. Former police officer Lloyd

Vipperman represented London during the hearing, contending that her works about Rolling were serious journalistic ventures and that the lien sought by the State amounted to an attack on the Bill of Rights.

"The only reason I'm being singled out is that Danny Rolling is so prominent and the families are so active," London asserted from her perch on the Speaker's Stone.

Christa Hoyt's mother, Ann Garren, stood nearby along with Diana Hoyt, Ricky and George Paules, and Ada Larson.

"I'm here to keep her from profiting from that book," Garren said. "It's a pornographic book."

"This is not a political issue," added Larson. "This is a criminal issue."

Another onlooker, Mark Kimbrel, had lived in Gainesville during Rolling's 1990 killing spree. He made no effort to hide his disgust for London.

"She's just a leech," Kimbrel sneered. "She's taking advantage of Rolling's situation for personal gain."

Later, after she finished her propaganda appearance and the reporters and other onlookers moved on to the next story demanding their attention, London walked with her attorney, Vipperman, across the parking lot. When they reached her car, an older model, dented, red Chevette, London shook Vipperman's hand.

"You're the best," she said with a sly smile. Vipperman had taken her case *pro bono*, free of charge, because he believed so greatly in the issue of free speech.

London started the engine and pulled out of the lot, turning the wrong way onto a one-way street. A sticker on her car's battered rear bumper read, *Practice random acts of kindness and senseless acts of beauty*.

Three weeks later, Judge Martha Ann Lott ruled on Florida's "Son of Sam" case, holding that since Sondra London was Rolling's "cyberspace" spouse and he had contractually granted her all rights in whatever literary or artistic works he created, the State could seize the profits she made from any artistic collaborations with him. London immediately planned to appeal the ruling.

Around the same time period, Rolling wrote to a student reporter at the *Independent Alligator*, responding to her letter asking how he felt about the death penalty:

> *I don't fear dying, Jaine. In a sense 5 life sentences to 170 years is a DEATH sentence in [and of] itself. A slow-death to be certain. This ain't living kid. It's barely existing.*
>
> *So . . . if the State of Florida is bound and determined to spend millions of dollars to put me in the HOT SEAT and call that justice, they're really doing me a favor.*
>
> *Like I said, I don't fear dying . . . I'm a Christian. I believe in our Lord & Savior Jesus Christ. So, if they ever do strap me in the chair I'll be home. This world is not my home. It has never been. My home is with Jesus.*
>
> *So there you have it, a whole page on how Danny feels about the Death Penalty.*

~~~~~
~~~~~

On September 28, 1999, the First District Court of Appeal in Tallahassee ruled on Sondra London's appeal of the trial court's order granting the State of Florida a lien against the proceeds of the works she collaborated on with Rolling. Citing the plain language of Florida's statutory provisions establishing the right to impose a civil restitution lien, which permitted such a lien against any "royalties, commissions, proceeds of sale, or any other thing of value accruing to the convicted offender, or a person on the convicted offender's behalf," the appellate court affirmed the lien against London. A few months later, a circuit court judge ordered that $15,000 seized via the lien would be transferred to the Crime Victims Compensation Fund.

Meanwhile, being behind bars day after day was taking its toll on Rolling. A March 2000 letter to one of his female pen pals offered a glimpse into Rolling's degenerating state of mind.

> *Going stir crazy. The walls, the motherfucking walls, are closing in. I am completely and absolutely miserable. Hell of a way to begin a letter. Now it's like I feel my face turns to stone. There is a cold that stabs through flesh and bone to freeze one's very soul. It is a Death Row prison cell.*
>
> . . . . .
>
> *I begin to see the handwriting on the wall. The only way to find release from the torment is to die. Let my spirit rise above the dismal life I endure in this life.*
>
> . . . . .

> *Doth not all eventually go the way of Earth? Once our eyes close to this world do they not open to the next?*

In a May 2000 interview conducted on Death Row with Tampa television station WFLA news anchor Stacie Schaible, Rolling insisted that an infernal force had demanded that he kill eight people to match the number of years he had spent in prison. He insinuated that he had killed Tom, Sean, and Julie Grissom prior to continuing his killing in Gainesville, but he stopped short of outright confessing to those additional three murders.

> Lucifer told me eight souls for every year I'd done in prison. When I got out of Parchman prison, that was eight years that I'd spent in prison, different prisons in the South. I've been convicted of five murders here in Florida. And then, well, you know, there's been, you know, talk that there were three others in Shreveport. And I'm sure you're aware of that.

Nodding his head in silent confirmation, he looked at Schaible with knowing eyes.

"That adds up to how many?" he asked rhetorically.

As he wrapped up the interview, Rolling stated that he expected to be executed and had come to terms with his fate.

"I've been preparing myself for years," he said with a smile. "God, I hope I go to heaven, because I've seen hell down here."

In early July, Rolling appeared in court to argue that his death penalty sentence should be reduced to a sentence of life imprisonment. Rolling told the judge that he received the death penalty only because his attorneys were incompetent in failing to get the case moved out of Gainesville. He claimed that his attorneys advised him that Gainesville was a good location for the trial because it was a liberal college town where he would be able to get an unbiased jury.

"I didn't feel comfortable about having the trial here," he asserted. "The people of Gainesville had been badly wronged. They looked at me from the viewpoint that I was a monster. I am not a monster."

In a lengthy letter to *The Associated Press* the following month, Rolling blamed the evil side of his personality for the murders that he committed ten years earlier.

> *When the night called, I could not resist its urgings. I knew it was wrong. When I looked into the mirror, the face I saw was my own, and I hated the things I had done.*
>
> *I lived a double, even triple life. One the pistol-wielding outlaw Ennad. The other I could not control, that of Gemini. I was possessed.*
>
> . . . . .
>
> *I assure you I am not a salivating ogre. Granted in time's past; the dark era of long ago – Dr. Jeckle [sic] & Mr. Hyde did strike up and down the corridors of insanity.*

He attributed his criminal acts to the incessant abuse from his father at home and the continual ill treatment that he received during his eight years of incarceration in Alabama, Georgia, and Mississippi.

> *A mangy dog gets more consideration than what I received in Parchman. Imagine being forced to dwell in a prison cell that floods out two to three times a week with putrefied raw sewage, and having to exist in such filth for over eight months till it drives you crazy as a loon.*

Rolling stated that he had pleaded guilty to the murders in hopes of receiving life imprisonment instead of the death penalty, and he discussed the reason for his appeal.

> *Why am I appealing my sentence? I am alive. I see. I hear. I touch, taste, feel as any human being attributes such gifts given by our creator. As long as the will to live remains, I stand on my feet.*
>
> *As to how many breaths remain in the soul of Danny Rolling, that is entirely in the sovereign will of God Almighty and the State of Florida.*

In closing, he seemed to convey remorse for his crimes.

> *Any complaint I may have pales in comparison to the terrible wrong I inflicted upon good people. I stand in the shadow of their suffering. If it is to be mercy, then I shall be eternally*

grateful. If it is to be the wrath of vengeance, then God grant me the strength to face what I must. For I owe a debt I cannot repay . . . not even with my own life.

~~~~~

Rolling received unexpected relief from his fear of Florida's electric chair. After several botched electrocution executions, including that of Allen Davis in 1999 when blood poured from his nose onto his shirt, the State of Florida changed its death penalty law. Beginning in 2000, criminals sentenced to death in Florida were given the choice of dying by the electric chair or lethal injection, widely perceived to be less painful. Virtually all have chosen lethal injection.
~~~~~

Chapter 24

Coping & Waiting

"*There is a war going on . . . between the forces of good and evil*" (Danny Rolling)

"*I let the evil in and the evil just took over*" (Danny Rolling)

As the ten-year anniversary of her daughter's murder approached, Ada Larson emailed *The Palm Beach Post*:

> *I was last in Gainesville on the 11th and 12th of July to attend the hearings on the killer's appeal for new trial. I try to attend all court appearances to do with this case. It is important for the court to know that we care as much today as ever.*
>
> *It is naturally emotional to keep reliving our tragedy. As the years have passed, the events have gotten less and less. I view this as an important anniversary. I want Sonja, Christi, Christa, Tracy and Manny to be remembered. It seems people always focus on the killer. It is also a good reminder for students that things like this can happen. They need to take every precaution.*
>
> . . . . .
>
> *I believe it is natural to think that tragedy always happens to someone else . . . I*

know you have to keep educating students. It can happen to them. I get upset when I see kids out alone at night. I just want to tell them, "Don't you know how dangerous that is?"

Sonja was a thoughtful, intelligent, fun-loving, caring and spirited individual who would have been a productive member of society. She could have been anything she wanted, as she had an aptitude for mathematics, she was a gifted artist, and had natural beauty. She loved children and wanted to work with them. She had many friends, and she was a great friend. The eighteen and one-half years I had with my daughter were the best years of my life.

Despite Larson's admonition about warning unwary students, Jamie Depelteau, a 21-year-old biology major at UF, reflected the perspective of the vast majority of his fellow students.

"It happened once and I'm sure it could happen again," he said, "but I don't think it will. I think things have probably evolved to prohibit that from happening again."

~~~~~

For part of its 10-year anniversary remembrance events, the City of Gainesville planted five palm trees in a median near the SW 34th Street wall. Each tree was paired with a nameplate: Sonja Larson, Christina Powell, Christa Hoyt, Manuel Taboada, and Tracy Paules. Nearly 50 members of the slain students' families attended a memorial dedication of the Wall and palm trees on August 25, 2000.
~~~~~

They thanked the law enforcement community and shared memories of their lost children.

"God, I remember where I was," said Frank Powell, recalling the moment he learned of his daughter's murder. "I'll never forget it. You better believe I'll never forget it. It's never been the same. It was my daughter and I loved her."

Less than an hour's drive away at Florida State Prison, Rolling's thoughts were not on remembering his victims. His emotions were not geared toward remorse or regret. Instead, only a week after the dedication ceremony in Gainesville, Rolling responded eagerly to an invitation from Rick Downey, originator of Mansonfamilypicnic.com, a website featuring letters and artwork by serial killers. In a letter dated August 31, 2000, Rolling wrote:

> *Hell-o Rick!*
>
> *Are you legit? I mean, are you for fucking real, dude? What man in his right mind would turn down an invitation to sling ink with hot & horny gals across the globe? I do get mail from chicks, but there's something about the way you put it.*
>
> *How did you put it:*
>
> *"I am swamped with pleas for your address & artwork. My female readers are becoming increasingly more desperate to have something from you. They think you're sexy, and my male readers are eager to provide you with plenty of photos of young girls wearing nothing more than a bikini. Yes, you'll have all of the*

youngest girls you could ever imagine, and I can help."

Well hell's bells & dragon's tails . . . COME ON DOWN!

Over in Orlando, Edward Humphrey was taking the next step towards regaining his life. Having been made out to be a monster by law enforcement, prosecutors, and the media for so long, nearly two years in all until a Gainesville grand jury found insufficient evidence to indict him, he endured whispers and stares from professors and classmates alike until, on August 5, the 28-year-old Humphrey graduated *magna cum laude* from the University of Central Florida, earning a Bachelor of Science degree in business administration with a 3.76 GPA.

"It's just another day," Humphrey said before the graduation ceremony, trying to downplay the significance of the event. "I did the work, I got it done, but there's a lot more ahead."

He had already overcome countless obstacles to get to that point. After putting himself through Brevard Community College and graduating with honors in 1994, Humphrey enrolled at UCF in 1995. He attended classes part-time and supported himself by working various jobs ranging from assembling tanning beds, to cleaning swimming pools, to working in factories.

His attorney, Donald Lykkebak, attended the graduation ceremony at UCF. Lykkebak felt an immense sense of satisfaction seeing Humphrey succeed after what he had been put through by the public and the press.

"Ed was in great, great danger because there were people willing to lie in order to be part of a story that was so much greater than they were," Lykkebak said. "They let the public believe that he was a demon."

Ellen Muniz, managing partner of a temporary employment service who helped Humphrey get several factory jobs, confirmed that he had performed well and received positive feedback from employers.

"He's really sweet," Muniz said. "He seems genuinely happy."

Lykkebak acknowledged that Humphrey blamed himself for not taking his manic-depressive medication during the time period that Rolling roamed the streets of Gainesville. However, like his client, he preferred to dwell on the positive.

"He has had to work hard to get where he is today, and he had a lot of distractions," Lykkebak said. "But you know, one thing about Ed Humphrey, he was an Eagle Scout. He's the kind of guy deep down who keeps working until he gets it done. And he did."

~~~~~

In the "In Memoriam" section of the April 24, 2001, edition of the *Shreveport Times*, Julie Grissom's mother published a poem to honor her birthday.

If we could have one

Lifetime wish

One dream come true

We would pray to God with

All our hearts for

Yesterday and you.

A thousand words can't

Bring you back

We know because we've tried

And neither will a million tears

We know because we've cried.
~~~~~

You left behind a broken heart

And happy memories too.

But we never wanted memories

We only wanted you.

To your resting place we go

The flowers are placed with care.

But no one knows the heartache

As we turn and leave you there.

~~~~~

In exchange for his testimony against Rolling, Bobby Lewis was transferred to a prison in Stillwater, Minnesota. He died there of hepatitis on July 22, 2001. His tongue-in-cheek obituary proclaimed that the *career criminal* had *escaped the confines of his earthly existence . . . after a lengthy illness*, and that although he made bad choices in life and *would often appeal to the worst in people, he did so in order to bring them together to achieve the best of results . . . He was most proud that his involvement in events following the Gainesville student murders spared the students' families a prolonged trial.*

~~~~~

Well into his sentence, clad in an orange prison jumpsuit and led into an interview room by two deputies, his leg shackles and handcuffs clicking and clanging with each step, Rolling attempted to explain what had driven him to murder innocent people.

> I let my guard down. I let the evil in and the evil just took over. It's like when the sun went down, I couldn't resist it. It would just pull like a tidal wave. And when the morning would come up, I'd hate

myself. It was like, "My God, what have I become." There was no turning back. And I think there's a war going on, and that war is in a dimension that you can't really see with your naked eye, between the forces of good and evil. Angels and devils, if you will, and they prey on us.

On www.mayhem.net, a website devoted to mass murder and serial killings, Rolling wrote to a teenager from Australia who posted that killers intrigued her:

> *I want you to listen to me very carefully. You mention you feel the thrill of the kill when you read stories about murder. If indeed that is the case, I strongly suggest you read something else. Why you might ask? Because KILLING of all deeds done by mortals is most tragic and horrible. Believe me, young lady, not only does the victim lose that which is more precious than silver or gold (LIFE). The KILLER loses a part of his or her soul every time a life is taken. God as my Sovereign Judge, I regret with all my mind, heart & soul that which I took. If only I could go back, I'd find a way to prevent what happened.*
>
> *I pray you NEVER find yourself on the other side of midnight dripping life blood of another. At that point you will have lost your way.*

One wonders whether Rolling would have taken the same remorseful tone had he never been caught. For his part, former State Attorney Rod Smith, now a state senator, remained steadfast in the belief that, given the chance, Rolling would gladly kill again.

"He talked about liking to look into the eyes at the point of death," Smith pointed out. "He could conquer and possess people who were far superior to him in terms of intellect and potential."

The five slain Gainesville students, and Julie Grissom before them, had attracted his attention because of their shared attributes, attributes he both coveted and resented.

"They were college students, they were ambitious, they were what he would never be. But for one night, he could control everything they were. Everything they would ever be."

As for the appropriateness of Rolling's execution, Smith stopped short of declaring the death penalty a perfect punishment, while still endorsing its application to Rolling.

"I can't, for a moment, answer whether or not it deters crime," he said. "Those issues are so difficult. What I can say is that I believe, then and now, that it will deter Danny Rolling. And that's enough for me."

~~~~~

On August 10, 2002, Edward Humphrey embarked on another new journey in his reclaimed life. At the Holy Name of Jesus Catholic Church in Indialantic, Humphrey married Graciela Moreno from Panama City, Panama. After honeymooning in Panama City, the couple started their new lives together in Palm Bay, Florida. Humphrey's beaming smile in a photograph accompanying the couple's wedding announcement revealed the depth of his new-found happiness and reflected the promise of a bright future.

~~~~~

As a Death Row inmate in Union Correctional Institute, Rolling was only allowed to leave his cell for approved visits, medical appointments, twice-a-week exercise sessions, and twice-a-week showers. Except for the exercise yard and shower, he stayed handcuffed for any excursions out of his cell. He spent the vast majority of his time in a non-air conditioned 6-by-9-by-9-foot cell with a stainless-steel toilet, sink, and bed. Like all Death Row inmates, Rolling wore an orange shirt and blue pants, ironically the same combination as the school colors for the University of Florida.

Rolling was not playing well with others as his stay on Death Row continued. Between 2000 and 2005, he fought with his fellow inmates in the exercise yard nearly every year, and prison records reflected that Rolling instigated each of the fights. Aside from the occasional fights, he stayed "pretty quiet," spending much of his time reading and watching TV.

John O'Ferrell, a former corrections officer who frequently encountered Rolling while patrolling Death Row, described him as "seeming like he was a regular person," an impression that struck him as odd considering the horrific crimes that Rolling had admitted committing.

~~~~~

On the other side of the country, unemployed actor and aspiring screenwriter Kevin Williamson was housesitting in Westwood, a small neighborhood near UCLA in Los Angeles, sitting on a sofa and channel surfing when he came across a TV special about the Gainesville student murders. The report of the killings both fascinated and frightened him. After watching the show, he began imagining a knife-wielding murderer watching him from outside the house, waiting in the darkness to strike.

The news story about the Gainesville slayings left such a lasting impression on Williamson that he ended up writing a screenplay based on the events. He sold the script
~~~~~

for *Scream* to the Weinstein Brothers production company for $400,000, and the resulting film went on to gross nearly $175 million worldwide, spawning a successful series of sequels as well.

~~~~~

While Rolling's legal team continued to pursue every available legal remedy on appeal, his time on Death Row dragged out longer and longer, much more than the average Death Row stay of 14 years, and much to the consternation of the families of his young victims.

"How much longer for these appeals?" asked Ada Larson, expressing the exasperation they all felt.

> It took two to three years for his last appeal, and just last month they denied it. They sent me like 40 pages from that hearing. I read the whole thing and it's just a lot of rehash of the same things. It's ridiculous.
>
> He's trying to get out of it by saying it's cruel and unusual punishment. How can it be cruel, considering what he did? It's a cakewalk compared to what he did. I think he ought to be stabbed as many times as he stabbed all his victims.

"Tracy had a bright future," Ricky Paules said, "and he took it all away. I'll pull the switch. I'll slit the throat, whatever, I'm ready," she said spitefully. "No mother should have to outlive her children."

On October 17, 2005, Richard Lucas of Gainesville wrote to the *Gainesville Sun*, his sarcastic tone no doubt conveying what many in the community felt.
~~~~~

Why is Danny Rolling still in prison? Maybe by now he is rehabilitated. Why don't we just let him out of prison? It would save the tax-paying people of Florida a lot of money. Every time his picture is on the front page he has such a remorseful look that I know he is sorry for killing five students. Maybe our governor could grant him a pardon.

Jeb, do your job. He has lived too long and too many people's lives have been ruined by this man. Expedite his execution.

Chapter 25

Ending a Nightmare

"The show must go on and I'm the VILLIAN" (Danny Rolling 3/12/94)

September 22, 2006, brought welcomed news to the families of Sonja Larson, Christi Powell, Christa Hoyt, Manny Taboada, Tracy Paules, Tom Grissom, Julie Grissom, and Sean Grissom. At long last, Florida Governor Jeb Bush signed a death warrant for Danny Rolling, paving the way for his sentence to be carried out:

> *NOW, THEREFORE, I, JEB BUSH, as Governor of the State of Florida and pursuant to the authority and responsibility vested in me by the Constitution and Laws of Florida, do hereby issue this warrant directing the Warden of the Florida State Prison to cause the sentence of death to be executed upon DANNY HAROLD ROLLING, in accordance with the provisions of the laws of the State of Florida.*

Rolling's execution date was scheduled for October 25.

"I'm thrilled," Ricky Paules said in reaction to the news. "I've been waiting to do this for 16 years. I hate to sound coarse about it, but that's the way I feel."

Dianna Hoyt, who vowed to attend the execution, voiced similar thoughts.

"I don't think there's any closure for something like this," she said. "But there is gratification to know that he can no longer think about the killings and get pleasure out of thinking about what he did. I really do believe that he deserves to be put to death; I want it to be over."

Tracy Paules's sister, Laurie Lahey, planned to attend the execution as well, but like Hoyt she did not expect it to provide any closure.

"I'm not looking forward to it," she said. "I have to do it for my sister. It's the last thing I can do for her."

Sonja Larson's mother, Ada, planned to witness the execution as well.

"I don't particularly want to do it," she said, "but it's something I have to do. For my daughter."

State Senator Rod Smith, the former prosecutor who had secured Rolling's death sentence so many years earlier, expressed disappointment that it had taken so long for the execution to be set, especially since Rolling had freely confessed to the killings and DNA evidence supported his confession.

"You understand why victims feel so frustrated by the justice system," Smith said.

With Rolling's death warrant finally a reality, his victims' families began their preparations, both emotionally and logistically, to attend the execution. Among those deciding whether to attend was Jim Larson, Sonja's brother. He had the unique position of awaiting two executions: one for Rolling and one for John Huggins, the man who had murdered his wife, Carla.

"I guess I would go," Larson said, referring to both felons' pending executions, "but I don't really care anymore. It's not going to be even. Those two lives don't compare to Carla's life, or Sonja's life."

Larson's new girlfriend understood the abrupt, senseless losses he had experienced. Her husband had died in a freak accident, killed when a tree fell on his Jeep.

She provided Larson much needed support, but he still struggled to stay positive, facing each day the best that he could.

"Everyone has this TV mentality," he explained, distinguishing the artificial smiles of sitcom actors from his somber reality. "It's not a happy ending. I don't feel good."

~~~~~

Wasting no time in their efforts to short-circuit the execution process, Rolling's attorneys filed a post-conviction motion on October 4, arguing that execution by lethal injection violated Rolling's constitutional right to be free from cruel and unusual punishment. But Rolling's final appeal to the Florida Supreme Court failed. On October 18, the court denied the appeal, utterly rejecting Rolling's claim that lethal injection "may subject the inmate to unnecessary pain."

~~~~~

As the date for Rolling's execution approached, satellite news trucks from CNN and local news stations for NBC, ABC, CBS, and other affiliates packed together in three or four rows, ten vehicles deep, outside Florida State Prison. On Wednesday, October 25, in a barren cow pasture across from the prison compound, a line of Florida Highway Patrol and Bradford County Sheriff's cruisers separated two groups of people gathered together. One group of about sixty death penalty supporters stood near a sign indicating "Supporters." Another slightly larger group demonstrating against capital punishment gathered by a sign that said "Opponents." Members of both groups chanted and carried their own hand-held signs with pro- or anti-death penalty slogans. One sign asserted: "We remember the victims . . . but not with more killing," while another read: "Whoever sheds man's blood by man, his blood shall be shed Genesis 9:6". Another proclaimed: "Finally . . . kill the killer". Yet another had a message for Rolling himself: "Danny this is 1. You owe us 4 more". Among those in the group against the death penalty was Atlanta attorney Hal Carter, Julie Grissom's former boyfriend.

"Whether it's by Danny Rolling or the state, it's murder," he said.

At 8:00 a.m. Danny Rolling met with his brother, Kevin, and the two said their farewells. After the three-hour goodbye, Rolling enjoyed a final meal of lobster tail, butterfly shrimp, baked potato, strawberry cheesecake, and sweet tea. He ate every last bite. Following his last meal, he took a shower and dressed in black pants, a white, long-sleeved shirt, and black shoes, and then returned to his cell. Reverend Mike Hudspeth, Rolling's designated spiritual advisor and the pastor of the United Pentecostal Church in Rolling's hometown of Shreveport, Louisiana, was the next to visit him. They talked for several hours through the bars of Rolling's cell, then a member of the execution team explained the lethal injection procedure to the condemned prisoner. Rolling remained "calm and cooperative" throughout the day. He had been given a dose of the tranquilizer, Librium, after his brother's visit.

~~~~~

Allison Kirkpatrick, a 22-year-old senior at UF, drove over from Gainesville with a friend to be outside Florida State Prison for Rolling's execution. Although only 6 at the time of the murders, Kirkpatrick had read about them after enrolling at the school.

"We feel connected to these murders," she said. "It was a random year, it was random people, but it could have been our year. It could have been us."

Tonya Wilson, friend of Sonja Larson and Christi Powell, voiced her anger about the mode of Rolling's execution.

"I'm an eye-for-an-eye kind of person. I think he's getting off so easy it's sickening."
~~~~~

Stephanie Cutshall, a UF student at the time of the murders and a petite brunette like the victims, expressed the same reaction.

"What he did was cruel and unusual. It was vicious. What they are doing to him, lethal injection, that's too humane."

~~~~~

At 5:30 p.m., the families of Rolling's victims were escorted into the execution chamber's viewing room along with official witnesses and members of the media. Nearly 50 chairs were crowded into five closely-packed rows, many more than what the room usually held. The families filled the first three rows, their individual and collective anguish palpable in the somber room. After strapping him to a gurney, execution team members wheeled Rolling into the execution chamber. Behind a large window covered with a brown curtain, they made final adjustments to the eight lethal injection syringes. The curtain rose at 5:59 p.m.

Secured to the gurney on his back, both arms extended on slats with a crisp white sheet covering his body from the neck down, Rolling turned his head slightly to glance through the glass window into the viewing room. His eyes seemed to pause when he saw Ricky Paules seated directly across the window from him, then he turned his head back up and gazed at the ceiling. Four prison guards stood around him, one behind his head, one by his side, and two behind his feet.

A microphone dangling above him was turned on.

"Danny Rolling, do you have a final statement?" a member of the execution team asked.

"Yes, I do," the condemned man replied.

Rolling closed his eyes and began to sing:
~~~~~

He who flung the stars into the heavens above,

Created the oceans, the mountains, the eagles and the doves.

None greater than Thee, Oh Lord,

None greater than Thee.

Angels bow before you and fold their wings

Lift your voice and praise the King of Kings.

None greater than Thee, Oh Lord,

None greater than Thee.

Thou art the alpha and omega

The beginning and the end.

At the sound of thy voice

Peace bestills the mighty wind.

None greater than Thee, Oh Lord,

None greater than Thee.

It was the same hymn he had sung thirty years earlier during his baptism at United Pentecostal Church. He sang in a clear, calm voice for nearly three minutes straight, then when he paused a moment, a prison official turned off the microphone. Rolling's lips began to move again, but as the big digital clock on the wall over his head displayed 6:03 p.m., a mixture of sodium pentothal, pancuronium bromide, and potassium chloride began to flow into Rolling's veins through an IV in his outstretched arm.

Rolling clenched his cheeks and then his face relaxed. His eyes rolled back in his head and then closed. His mouth stopped moving. Then at 6:11 p.m., his chest heaved for the final time. The color slowly left his face, going from red to ashen and then to the pale-blue of the dead. The lethal cocktail of drugs knocked him unconscious and paralyzed him before stopping his heart, sending him into oblivion to meet the force that had forged his fragmented soul.

Outside the prison walls, the pro-death penalty crowd started clapping in unison, celebrating that the deadly cocktail was flowing through Rolling's veins. Inside the execution chamber, a physician covered by a hood bent over Rolling's unmoving body with a stethoscope. One minute later, a second doctor did the same. The microphone came back on in the witness chamber. A voice on the speaker declared Danny Harold Rolling dead at 6:13 p.m. Then the brown curtain silently closed. After 4,571 days, Rolling's time on Death Row had ended.

A mass of people outside cheered in unison when they heard the sound of a large bell confirming that Rolling's sentence had been carried out. They clapped and cheered again when the white hearse carrying Rolling's body drove out of the prison compound around 6:30 p.m. in the fading light of dusk. A few feet away, a contingent from the other group stood solemnly in a circle and sang "Amazing Grace." After a while, the members of both crowds began to disperse, silently walking back to their cars, heading back to their normal lives.

Hal Carter left gravely disappointed, not just because he opposed the death penalty, but because he had hoped that Rolling would confess to killing Tom, Sean, and Julie Grissom. He was convinced that Rolling had committed the murders, and Rolling himself had hinted at it, but without a full confession, neither he nor the Grissom family could ever be completely certain. Carter had gone so far as to write Rolling several weeks earlier asking him for the "truth about the Grissom murders." Rolling replied by assuring him, "You will be vindicated. My word."

Hours before Rolling's execution, as Carter stood outside in the crowd of death penalty opponents, something remarkable had happened. A sparrow fell from the sky and landed at his feet. He gently picked the bird up and cradled it in his hands throughout the execution. Even more remarkable was what had happened after the pronouncement of Rolling's death. Carter raised the sparrow above his head and opened his hands, and the bird hesitated only a moment before soaring into the sky.

~~~~~

For the families of the murdered students, the long wait was finally over, the nightmare had finally ended. After being escorted out of the witness chamber, the parents and siblings of Rolling's victims expressed relief mixed with other emotions.

"I didn't understand how after what he did he could sit there and talk about the angels watching over him," said Diana Hoyt. "I'm a nurse, and I've seen my patients die. And they died a much more horrific death than what this man suffered through, that's for sure. He relaxed, went to sleep, did not feel anything." The resentment in her voice was unmistakable.

Joyce Burton, Julie Grissom's mother, echoed Hoyt.

"I witnessed his execution and it was nothing compared to what he put his victims through," she said. "At least I can get up knowing he's not breathing the air that our children should still be breathing. We will never have closure on this, until we close our eyes – all of us parents – for the last time, but thank God we had great kids, we have great memories, and that's what keeps me going."

Ada Larson expressed a similar reaction.
~~~~~

“It was a very easy, humane way to die. I could see when he stopped breathing. I thought, ‘Good riddance. You’re history.’”

“I think it was too easy on him,” added Zachary Thompson, brother of Sean Grissom. “But what can you do? He’s gone now, and I’m thankful for that.”

It was the first execution that Alachua County State Attorney Bill Cervone had ever attended. One time was enough for him to make up his mind about them.

“My bottom-line feeling is the punishment doesn’t fit the crime,” he said. “I’m sitting there watching that and running through my mind is what I know he did to those kids. To watch his death in such an antiseptic and clinical environment convinces me that the punishment does not fit that crime.”

Retired Gainesville police officer Gary Manning was among the crowd gathered outside. He had been one of the first responders to the scene of the Sonja Larson and Christi Powell murders.

“The Bible says, ‘An eye for an eye’,” he said solemnly. “I believe justice was done today.”

Baya Harrison, Rolling’s appellate lawyer, expressed regret that his client had not apologized to the victims’ families.

“I was hoping he would have repeated to them what he told me, that he was very remorseful. I think that’s what a lot of those family members were hoping for, and they deserved it.”

Laurie Lahey alternated between relief and tears.

“To watch him disappear, I feel a lot better now,” she said.

In a prepared statement handed out to the media, Ada Larson expressed relief tempered with enduring loss.

> *Our pain will never go away, but this evil man has gone away now. He will no longer gain sympathy from those who have befriended him while in prison. He will no longer be able to draw his illicit and weird drawings. He will no longer be housed, fed, and taken care of on our expense. He could die 8 times, as would have been more just. His life does not equal the lives he took.*

Manny Taboada's brother, Mario, decided against attending the execution.

"I felt nothing good would come from witnessing this," he said in a tone still projecting the pain of his loss.

That night CNN talk show host Nancy Grace devoted her program to Rolling's execution. Outraged that he had tried to prevent or postpone his execution by claiming that lethal injection amounted to cruel and unusual punishment, Grace turned to the attorneys on her panel.

Grace:	I'd like to hear you tell me with a straight face . . . why this guy should not have gotten the death penalty.
Attorney:	I'm not here to defend this guy or what he did. He's certainly a horrible, horrible human being. But our system was designed to be

better than that. In fact, our system was designed that we would rather let 100 guilty men go free than ever execute one innocent person. A system that . . .

Grace: Ok, whoa, whoa, whoa, whoa, wait! I don't even know what you're talking about. That doesn't even apply here. We're not talking about innocent people being convicted. We're not talking about guilty people being free. I'm talking specifically to you about the allegation that lethal injection, which is sodium pentothal, pancuronium bromide and potassium chloride, is cruel and unusual. Just a simple question, looking for a simple answer.

Death penalty expert Robert Blecker from New York Law School was quick to add his opinion.

> It's a terrible method because it too much resembles a hospital. It too much resembles the way we put to sleep those we love who are suffering from incurable and incredibly painful illnesses. Yes, it's cruel and unusual, it's cruel to the victims' families that he should go out the way he went out, when his victims went out the way they went out.
>
> If ever the death penalty is justified, this is the case.
>
> . . . . .
>
> This person deserves it by virtue of what he did, by virtue of how he did it, and most of all, by virtue of the suffering that he inflicted and the experience that the victims had.

Grace challenged an assertion by Sarah Craft, head of an anti-death penalty group: "Can you give me the name of one person executed in Florida that was later exonerated?"

"No," Craft replied, "I cannot."

Later in the show, Blecker recounted a visit he had made to Florida's death row where one of the guards described seeing Rolling for the first time. The brutal rapist and cold-blooded killer of eight was "playing volleyball with his shirt off and oiled up with suntan lotion." The outraged Blecker continued by recalling when he himself first saw Rolling lying in bed in his cell, propped up on pillows with a lamp casting light over his shoulder with a content look on his face. He was engrossed in a book, enjoying his own little world.

~~~~~

After his execution, Danny Rolling was buried in the Florida State Prison Cemetery in Raiford, Florida. In the days that followed, the death penalty debate continued. Posters on Deadsilence, a blog about serial killers, voiced some of the most common conflicting views about the event. On October 26, "Save Danny Rolling" wrote:

> *When someone can explain to me how the killing of another human – for whatever reason – makes sense, some 2006 years after the death of Christ, I would like to hear it.*
>
> *Ask yourself, are we killing another human being with malice aforethought? If the answer is yes, then it is murder. You cannot justify murder for any reason or you bear the same scars as the evildoer.*
>
> *Florida should stay all executions, especially Rolling's, or bear the burden of its sins.*

A poster named "James" disagreed:

> *I am a 23 year old cop from Gainesville, FL. I personally felt compelled to be standing outside the prison when the execution occurred . . . Danny Rolling was a monster, an animal, and I am happy to now be able to say his name in the PAST tense. I clapped alongside*
~~~~~

> *my parents, girlfriend, younger brother and sister, and others from my community as he was pronounced DEAD. We also cheered as the hearse drove away. When an animal is rabid or sick, you PUT IT DOWN . . . He's finally received his punishment and the souls of those brutally removed from this earth can rest, along with their families. I know every breath of air I breathe will be a little sweeter knowing that Dannyboy is gone.*

"Charles Strozier" provided some insight into why Rolling may have turned out the way he did:

> *I am the first cousin of Danny by marriage through Aunt Claudia. I feel sad for my aunt who never had a chance to enjoy a peaceful life because of James Harold Rolling. You are right about Danny not being able to get help from anyone. If Aunt Claudia could have only left James Harold for good when Danny was a child and found help for him things would have been different . . . The Shreveport Police Department back then only protected James Harold from his crazy insane ways and covered up any beatings and abuse that he inflicted on Danny, Kevin, or Aunt Claudia. Now Kevin is the only*

one left to deal with what happened to his family. My prayers are with him always.

"Criminal Justice student," posting many months later, offered additional perspective:

What Rolling did was terrible. But there is a point in what you are saying about abuse. It really does things to people. Now to me it seems as if he deflected his resentment towards his mother by viciously murdering women in particular. I think that he resented his mother for letting the abuse go on and for not taking him away from his father for good. Now what is so fascinating to me is the question, what is it in some abused people that makes them want to kill? I, being the victim of abuse as a child, would never think to murder anyone. I see the wrong in abuse and it saddens me. What made Danny Rolling go the other way? It is interesting to study . . .

The questions and debate seemed doomed to continue indefinitely.

~~~~~

Back in Shreveport, Louisiana, Reverend Mike Hudspeth revealed that shortly before his execution Rolling had slipped Hudspeth a letter confessing to the three Grissom murders committed in 1989. Hudspeth read Rolling's letter at the Shreveport Police Department on the morning of October 27.
~~~~~

> *In order to fulfill all things that no stone be unturned. Here by I make a formal written statement concerning the murders of Julie, Tom & SEAN GRISSOM in my hometown of Shreveport, Louisiana . . . HAL CARTER, Julie Grissom's former fiancée [sic] is 100% INNOCENT – TOTALLY PURE of that crime. I, and I alone, am guilty. It was my hand that took those precious lights out of this ole dark world. With all my heart & soul would I could bring them back. Being a native son of Shreveport, I can only offer this confession of deep felt remorse over the loss of such fine -- outstanding souls.*

He insisted that Rolling "appeared very humble and regretful" when he submitted the written confession just before being taken to the execution chamber. Hudspeth also disclosed that Rolling had told him over a decade earlier that he killed the Grissoms, but pastor confidentiality rules required that he keep the confession to himself.

In response to the confession, Scott Grissom, Sean's father, released a statement: *Danny Rolling was the monster we all fear. It's the thought that he no longer walks this earth that gives me some sort of release. My Dad, Julie and Sean would not want have wanted us to let this pull us to the bottom. They would want us all to go on with our lives, be happy and blessed.*

Now Hal Carter had the certainty he so desperately wanted.

"Not only was I destroyed over Julie's death," he recalled of the days immediately following the murders, "I was also falsely accused. Worst of all, the real killer was free to strike again." Now a weight had been lifted from him. Rolling's confession not only "changed a very sad day, but also the rest of my life."

He thanked God for the confession, but surprisingly, someone else as well.

"I also thanked Danny," he said. "I know he was a terrible killer, but he kept his word."

I know that sorrow, that heartfelt bane, that dross th' mortal flame. Stone 'pon stone th' final throw ... etched hither tow – th' captive soul.

- Danny Rolling -

In order to fulfill all things that no stone be unturned. Here by I make a formal written statement concerning the murders of Julie, TOM & SEAN GRISSOM in my hometown of Shreveport, LOUISIANA ... HAL CARTER, Julie Grissom's former fiancel is 100% INNOCENT – TOTALLY PURE of that crime I, and I alone am guilty. It was my hand that took those precious lights out of this ole dark world. With all my heart & soul would I could bring them back. Being a native son of Shreveport, I can only offer this confession of deep felt remorse over the loss of such fine – outstanding souls

Have wept an ocean of Tears ... By which mournful doth float 'pon a sea of regret.

Danny Rolling!

D.R.

~~~~~

Bill Maxwell held the unenviable position of knowing two of Rolling's victims. Maxwell's sister had been the girls' volleyball coach at Ely High School in Pompano Beach, and one of her best players was Sonja Larson. He met Sonja on several occasions at his sister's house when she had the
~~~~~

volleyball team over for barbeques. As a professor at Santa Fe Community College in Gainesville in 1990, he had befriended Christa Hoyt while she was a student there. He came to know her better through frequent trips with his daughter to the video store in Archer where Christa worked. The first time he took his daughter to rent a Pippi Longstocking video, Christa had complimented her long hair. After that, he often left his daughter at the store so Christa could braid her hair. Now, he wrestled with what to tell his daughter about why Christa was no longer around, just as he struggled with the question of why two young lives had been so abruptly snuffed out. A journalist friend of his attended Rolling's execution and tried to help him make sense of what had happened.

"As I stared into the execution chamber, I felt his isolation and outsiderness," she told him. "I didn't have anything in common with him. Nobody did. It was like he wasn't human. He was a nobody – a nothing. But everybody knew this nobody's name. I just wish he had not existed."

Chapter 26

Healing & Remembering

"We have shared a story about sorrow . . . but we also shared a story about hope"

(Statement from the murdered students' families)

Richard Ward, a key leader of the Gainesville Task Force, died on October 21, 2009. He had devoted 28 years of his life to the Gainesville Police Department, surviving long after doctors diagnosed him with lung cancer. He was proud of his work investigating the five student murders.

"He looked at it as putting together a puzzle," his daughter said. "He was a man who loved justice and truth."

~~~~~

Janet Frake, the only known survivor of one of Rolling's rage-induced rapes, died after a three-year battle with throat cancer on June 11, 2012. She was 51.

~~~~~

James Harold Rolling, the source of a serial killer's deep psychological scars and inextinguishable inner rage, died on December 20, 2012, at the age of 81. He outlived his infamous eldest son by six years.

~~~~~

On the hot, sunny summer afternoon of August 25, 2015, the families and friends of Sonja, Christi, Christa, Manny, and Tracy gathered with members of the Gainesville community under the cathedral ceiling of the University of Florida's Baughman Center overlooking a small, tree-lined lake for a memorial ceremony. Five vases displaying white flowers formed a semi-circle around the podium at the front
~~~~~

of the Center's chapel area. The ceremony began with Hannah Huff, a graduate student at the University of Florida, singing an emotional rendition of "Somewhere Over the Rainbow." Then UF President Kent Fuchs addressed the assembly.

Expressing his admiration for the family members for "being a beacon of strength to all parents and family members who have endured the loss of their children," Fuchs referenced the memorial mural on the 34th Street wall. He emphasized how the college and community had come together "united in grief and support" during the "dark days of 1990" and stressed the importance of recognizing how "human spirit overcame evil."

During her turn at the podium, Sadie Darnell, now the Sheriff for Alachua County, recited the names of the five lost students and asserted that "each of them was unique, special, and brought such promise to our world." Wearing a white ribbon on her uniform, Sheriff Darnell stated that "there are no words to explain why" their young lives were so violently and prematurely snuffed out. She described how the horrific events of August 1990 in such a "pristine and beautiful place" had forced everyone to see the world differently and "recognize that horrible things can happen to bright and vibrant individuals," but that it had also revealed their community "at its finest hour." Then she read a statement from the victims' families, pausing at times to keep her composure:

> It is here that we brought our children to their college careers. It is here that we lost them to murder. It is here that we come to remember them.
>
> With you we have shared a story about sorrow, living in fear, losing trust, and being lost in pain. But then we also shared a

> story about hope, about letting go, about lifelines, and survival. We have found strength in you and continue to be soothed by you and by your presence in our grief. We hope that you will remember August 1990 without any sense of community shame for what happened here.
>
> On behalf of the mothers, the fathers, the siblings, the nieces, nephews, and friends within whom they now exist, you have affected us deeply. It is with pride that we remember our children, Sonja, Christi, Christa, Manny, and Tracy, and the community which first took care of them, and then took care of us.

After Sheriff Darnell, Diana Hoyt stepped carefully to the podium. She conveyed the families' gratitude for everyone helping to keep the memories of their children alive, a simple act which she said "means so much to us." She explained that "The Wall" had given the families something tangible to help them in the grieving process by letting them see the "wonderful names of their children," and giving them a place to go and reflect about their loss. She expressed appreciation for the fact that the wall had been preserved and maintained for over two decades, concluding by emphasizing that "we cherish this remembrance and it's with heartfelt gratitude that we thank all of you."

Patricia Powell spoke after Hoyt, recalling how a "demonic person was roaming loose destroying young people's lives," before going on to detail the lasting effects of Christi Powell's death on all of her siblings, nieces, and nephews, most of whom were in attendance that day at the memorial ceremony. Powell remarked that Rolling had been so "rotten through and through" that his rotten tooth that had to be removed helped to identify him as the killer, and she stressed that while their family would never forget what happened, "we are healed and everyone is living a good, normal life."

The ceremony concluded with a prayer of remembrance: "Dear God of Healing and Comfort . . . today we remember that there is a wall of "glorious impermanence" that is more than a wall, it is a symbol . . . and as the wounds continue to be healed, we stand here because we will always remember."

Among the attendees was Verlinda McDaniel. She had been one of the jurors who recommended a death sentence for Rolling, and she came to the ceremony to pay her respects to the families.

"I've always felt connected to them and this terrible tragedy," she said. "I don't regret my decision to this day," she added, referring to her part in the jury's decision. "I don't think I've ever felt so angry in my life," she recalled of the time she spent evaluating the evidence at trial. "My heart just went out to the family."

When he heard about the memorial ceremony, Adam Tritt, the original creator of the slain students' mural at the Wall, expressed astonishment about its longevity.

"I never expected it to be maintained for 25 years," he said, "it's pretty amazing."

~~~~~

Despite investigators' best efforts, the murder weapons used in the Gainesville student slayings and in the Shreveport killings – Rolling's Ka-Bar knives -- were never recovered.

As for Rolling himself, the depravity of his deeds still shocks the senses, demanding our attention.
~~~~~

“He’s in the classification of Bundy or Wuornos,” Rod Smith pronounced. “He will forever have a certain infamous notoriety.”

“Absolutely the worst crime scenes I’ve ever seen,” echoed Lt. LeGran Hewitt of the Alachua County Sheriff’s Office. “It’s not a case that’s going to ever be forgotten.”

~~~~~

Many, perhaps most, of the current students in Gainesville have only a vague idea about what happened in August 1990 when a deranged serial killer murdered five of their predecessors. To the current generation of students, the name Danny Rolling exists as something less than a memory, some distant fact of history no more real to them than fading photos of Ted Bundy. When they first see the slain students’ names listed on the 34th Street wall, they may pause a moment to wonder what lives are honored there. But they are young and invincible. They will live forever. The moment of reflection does not last.

However, there are still those in the community who understand the lasting effects of traumatic events. They know what happened so many Augusts ago. Spencer Mann, former Alachua County Sheriff’s Office spokesman, is one of them.

“I think the impact is greater on the permanent Gainesville residents than the students because it was part of the fabric of our history,” he says.

Gainesville Police Chief Sadie Darnell is another who believes in the importance of memory. She suggests that those who forget the past are doomed to repeat it.

“It could happen anywhere, at any time,” Darnell cautions, “and it will happen again somewhere.”

But Darnell insists that the good be recognized along with the bad. She notes that out of the darkness of the Gainesville killings came light.
~~~~~

"I think we are a stronger community because of it," she points out. "Instead of hunkering down and hiding, our community pulled together and looked out for each other."

Intended to "honor their memory and to perpetuate their aspiration," the 1990 Student Memorial Scholarship and the Sonja Larson Memorial Scholarship are one way the community helps to ensure that the five murdered students' names live on. In addition to honoring the victims, the scholarships have provided more than 300 students nearly half a million dollars in financial awards at the University of Florida.

But a more visible symbol of the community's shared consciousness is the memorial panel on the 34th Street wall. Despite the passage of time, the years now grown into decades, the Wall has endured, ensuring that the loss of five young lives will not be forgotten. It continues to memorialize Sonja Larson, Christina Powell, Christa Hoyt, Manuel Taboada, and Tracy Paules with a simple but essential message: "*REMEMBER*".

Appreciation

Thank you to my editor, proofreaders, and cover artist for your support:

Aeternum Designs (book cover); Bettye McKee (editor); Katherine McCarthy, Robyn MacEachern, Kathi Garcia, Sandra Miller, and Lee Husemann

~ JT

Enjoy this book? You can make a big difference.

Reviews are one of the most powerful tools when it comes to book ranking, exposure and future sales. I have a bunch of loyal readers, and honest reviews of my books help bring them to the attention of other readers.

If you've enjoyed this book, I would be very grateful if you'd take a few minutes to write a brief review on Amazon.

Thank you so much,

JT

About the Author

JT Hunter is an attorney with over fifteen years of experience practicing law, including criminal law and appeals, and he has significant training in criminal investigation techniques. He is also a college professor in Florida where his teaching interests focus on the intersection of criminal psychology, law, and literature.

JT is the bestselling author of *The Devil In The Darkness*, *The Vampire Next Door: The True Story of The Vampire Rapist John Crutchley* *Deadly Deception*, *Death Row Romeo* and *The Country Boy Killer: The True Story of Serial Killer Cody Legebokoff*

Other Books by JT Hunter

DEVIL IN THE DARKNESS

Optioned May 2018 by a Major Production Company to be made into a Motion Picture

He was a hard-working small business owner, an Army veteran, an attentive lover, and a doting father. But he was also something more, something sinister. A master of deception, he was a rapist, arsonist, and bank robber, and a new breed of serial killer, one who studied other killers to perfect his craft. He methodically buried kill-kits containing his tools of murder years before returning to reclaim them. Viewing the entire country as his hunting grounds, he often flew across the country to distant locations where he would rent a car and drive hundreds or even thousands of miles before randomly selecting his victims. Such were the methods and madness of serial killer Israel Keyes. Such were the demands of the 'Devil in the Darkness'.

Amazon Links - eBook | Paperback | Audiobook

THE COUNTRY BOY KILLER

He was the friendly, baby-faced, Canadian boy next door. He came from a loving, caring, and well-respected family. Blessed with good looks and backwoods country charm, he was popular with his peers, and although an accident at birth left permanent nerve damage in one of his arms, he excelled in sports. A self-proclaimed "die hard" Calgary Flames fan, he played competitive junior hockey and competed on his school's snowboarding team. And he enjoyed the typical simple pleasures of a boy growing up in the country: camping, hunting, and fishing with family and friends. But he also enjoyed brutally murdering women, and he would become one of the youngest serial killers in Canadian history.

THE VAMPIRE NEXT DOOR

While he stalked the streets hunting his unsuspecting victims, the residents of a quiet Florida town slept soundly, oblivious to the dark creature in their midst, unaware of the vampire next door.

John Crutchley seemed to be living the American Dream. Good-looking and blessed with a genius level IQ, he had a prestigious, white-collar job at a prominent government defense contractor, where he held top secret security clearance and handled projects for NASA and the Pentagon. To all outward appearances, he was a hard-working, successful family man with a lavish new house, a devoted wife, and a healthy young son.

But he concealed a hidden side of his personality, a dark secret tied to a hunger for blood and the overriding need to kill. As one of the most prolific serial killers in American history, Crutchley committed at least twelve murders, and possibly nearly three dozen. His IQ eclipses that of Ted Bundy, and his body count may have as well.

DEATH ROW ROMEO

Three young women abducted and brutally murdered. For years, their killer remained a mystery as the cases turned cold. Then a Crime Stoppers call led to his arrest. Charming and handsome, serial killer Oscar Ray Bolin married a member of his legal defense team, and he toyed with the criminal courts for decades while on Death Row.

This is the first book written about Oscar Ray Bolin and his victims.

DEADLY DECEPTION

WARNING: This book contains several crime scene photos that are graphic in nature and may be very disturbing to some people. Do not proceed if under the age of 18 or are disturbed by scenes of death and violence.

One after another, young women disappeared without a trace in the night. One by one, their brutalized bodies turned up, the macabre crime scenes suggesting they shared the same cruel fate. Abducted, bound, and raped, all fell prey to an unknown killer, all became the victims of a deadly deception.

Amazon Links - eBook | Paperback | Audiobook

RJ Parker Publishing, Inc.

Experience a thought-provoking and engrossing read with books from RJ Parker Publishing. Featuring the work of crime writer and publisher RJ Parker, as well as many other authors, our company features exciting True CRIME and CRIME Fiction books in eBook, Paperback, and Audiobook editions.

Sources

1. *Witness statements, investigative reports, Student Homicide Task Force meeting minutes, correspondence, and other police files from the Alachua County Sheriff's Office, the Gainesville Police Department, and the Florida Department of Law Enforcement.*

2. *Correspondence between Danny Rolling and Sondra London and correspondence between Robert Lewis and Sondra London obtained via public records requests.*

3. *Deposition transcripts and hearing transcripts in State of Florida v. Danny Harold Rolling, Case Nos. 90-14200, 91-01932, 91-05620, 91-05621 (Hillsborough County Circuit Court); and in State of Florida v. Danny Harold Rolling, Case No. 91-03832 (Alachua County Circuit Court).*

4. *FBI witness interviews obtained via the Freedom of Information Act.*

5. *Clinton Police Department police reports Case No. 85-3624 & 85-3628.*

6. *Mississippi Department of Corrections records regarding Danny Rolling, MDOC No. 62065, Parchman State Penitentiary.*

7. *Danny Rolling statement to WFTV, https://www.youtube.com/watch?v=hDiVAUz5Jyo, retrieved May 10, 2018.*

8. *Deadsilence blogsite, http://deadsilence.wordpress.com, retrieved February 28, 2018.*

9. *Newspaper articles from the St. Petersburg Times, Gainesville Sun, Florida Today, Palm Beach Post, New York Times, Shreveport Times, Miami Herald, and Orlando Sentinel (1989-2016).*

10. *Ka-Bar Knives website, https://www.kabar.com/products/1320 , retrieved 5/22/18.*

11. *Kunen, James. "A Killer on the Campus". People.com (9/17/90), retrieved 5/18/18.*

12. *Mackenzie, Margaret. Courting the Media: Public Relations for the Accused and the Accuser. Praeger Publishers: Westport, CT (2007).*

13. *Maples, William R. Dead Men Do Tell Tales. Doubleday: New York (1994).*

14. *Rolling, Danny & Sondra London. The Making of a Serial Killer. Feral House: Portland, OR (1996).*

Made in the USA
Coppell, TX
14 December 2019

12943180R00164